Travels of Faith

Travels of Faith

Faith Annette Sand

Foreword by Arthur F. Glasser

Erika Oller, Illustrator

HOPE
Publishing House
P.O. Box 60008
Pasadena, CA 91106

Several of the chapters of this book have appeared in different forms, as follows: Chapter 5 as "The Andean Marauders," *The Other Side*, July 1980; Chapter 7 as "The Motilone Miracle," *The Other Side*, June 1981; Chapter 8 as "A *Favela* Parish," *Revista Maryknoll*, June 1983; and Chapter 9 as "Guatemalan Unrest—An Unpredictable Volcano," *World Vision*, October 1982. Used by permission.

Library of Congress Cataloging in Publication Data
Sand, Faith Annette, 1939–
    Travels of Faith.

    1. Sand, Faith Annette, 1939-   . 2. Christian biography— United States.
3. Christianity and justice— Developing countries. 4. Developing countries—
Church history. I. Title.

BR1725.S265A38 1985   270.8'2   85–17751

ISBN 0–932727–03–4

For Heather and Heidi —
traveling companions who have brought incredible joy to my life.

Contents

Foreword

Every so often there comes into one's circle of friends a person whose impact is different. Not just supportive, but challenging. Not just reassuring, but probing. Such a person is Faith Annette Sand. My wife Alice and I have not been the same since she invaded our lives.

I recall the first day we met. It was in the dean's office of the School of World Mission. There she was— tall, open, direct, and very intelligent— an "MK"* with 15 years of missionary experience behind her in Brazil. I later met her two charming daughters and learned of the eight Brazilian orphans that she raised in her own home.

You can be sure that I consider it a privilege to write this foreword and commend this book to the widest possible reading constituency. Over the years Alice and I have spent many happy hours with Faith and her husband Al. Our most recent and most memorable jaunt was a two week trip through central Spain. Of course, Faith had lived there years before! She knew all the really important sites we had to see and the things we had to do. She was our interpreter in every way and you can imagine the enrichment that came to us through this journey with Faith. We've truly seen her in action. And it is action par excellence!

We have been impressed with the authenticity of her commitment to Jesus Christ, the depth of her concern for all dimensions of the human condition, and the ability she has of seeing through the fog of the average Christian's thought and action (of people's too!). She can discern with uncanny skill the real issues and the nubs around which great questions turn. No breathless pursuit of the latest theological novelties. No courting of popularity at the expense of integrity. No easy capitulation to the status quo. So far as Faith is concerned, it's okay to be different when your intentions are positive and constructive and loving!

The Head of the Church has made comprehensive provision for the total ministry of his people. He has given to his people pastors and teachers to provide for their Christian nurture. Where would

*missionary kid.

iii

the Church be without its shepherds! He has also equipped some Christians with an apostolic-evangelistic-missionary gift to lead the Church in its outreach, serving as his spokespersons to the unbelieving world. Where would the Church be without those who pry Christians loose from mere "maintenance" activity and get them to face outward with the message of Jesus Christ! Where would we be if no one had spoken to us of Him!

But there is another dimension to the Christian ministry that is neither pastoral nor evangelistic. And here is where Faith serves. True, she has a good track record when it comes to sharing the gospel, stressing the necessity of personal commitment to Christ and building up the saints. But when I think of her sharp mind, perceptive eye and facile pen coupled with her heightened sense of truth and justice, I cannot but conclude that God has given her a uniquely prophetic ministry.

And you know what this means. One has only to recall the anguish of the Old Testament prophets—their obedience to God, their loyalty to truth, their courage in the face of compromise, the ostracism and suffering they endured, and their concern for the integrity and ongoing of God's redemptive purpose in history. On occasion I have seen Faith display first one and then another of these demanding qualities. Friends have been greatly helped by her insights. The careless have been rebuked by her faithfulness. Some of the encapsulated have been hurt by her witness. But I have only stood back and recalled a statement I read somewhere that on occasion even the words of Jesus Christ hurt and offend—because we tolerate things in our lives that He must hurt and offend until they are candidly recognized for what they are, and put away, once and for all.

Do enjoy this journey with Faith! You will be enriched. You'll agree: It's okay to be different—and you will thank God for those in our day who like Faith stand against all the false values and cant of our generation—a generation that seems so bent on its own self-destruction.

—**Arthur F. Glasser**, Dean Emeritus
and Senior Professor of Theology
and East Asia Studies
School of World Mission,
Fuller Theological Seminary
Pasadena, California

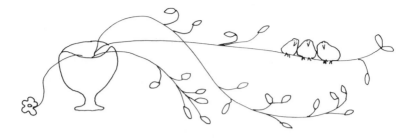

Introduction

I come by my wanderlust honestly. When I was a chubby three-month old baby, my great-aunt, an elderly Norwegian immigrant, announced to my parents that it might be all right for them, but they had no right to caper off around the world exposing me to unknown risks. World War II was then making all international travel precarious, and Aunt Hilda decreed it immoral to subject a baby to the rigors of the mission field.

No one in the family has ever been renowned for taking advice, so my parents, true to genetic form, continued on with their plans made while my mother was still in the hospital recovering from birthing me. I had been named Faith because during those days they decided to leave their safe Lutheran pastorate in Minneapolis and join that interesting genre of faith missionaries.

In spite of Aunt Hilda's warning, I was bundled away from the placid, tree-lined lakeshore community in south Minneapolis where all my cousins were to grow up. Shortly thereafter we landed in Toronto, Canada, and began a spartan English-styled life which is apparently peculiar to those wishing to candidate for missionary life.

The easy mobility of the missionary community meant that in the next three years we had lived in Pittsburgh, Pennsylvania; San Antonio, Texas; and Seattle, Washington. My earliest memories are from San Antonio where I recall the excitement I felt waking up

1

to the celebration of my third birthday. I also remember the marvels of watching my father build a little wood frame church for the Spanish-speaking congregation there (missionary candidates learn varied skills!).

Most of my childhood memories centered around mobility. There was that blue cellophane which we put over the headlights driving down the coast from Seattle to Los Angeles. World War II had started and a submarine attack was imminent, everyone felt, so we chugged down the coast highway in our 1936 black Oldsmobile sedan, camouflaged from terrorific attackers.

We stayed awhile in Los Angeles waiting for a wartime rarity—a neutral ship which could carry us to our assigned post in South America. At four, I was growing into understanding, but I can still recollect the bafflement and awe I felt when the militia vans came rolling into the neighborhood. The tailgate was lowered into a platform and we were herded around to watch a pretty girl urge us all to save tin cans and grow vegetables for the war effort. Even though I never quite made the connection between cans and war, I can remember still how much she looked like a monkey when she demonstrated to us how to wear a gas mask.

Finally an Argentine passenger liner with the large, spotlighted red cross on its side (which supposedly proclaimed its neutrality to all nefarious types) came our way, and a few months later we landed in the Andean valley of Colombia, South America, which nestled the city of Medellin, the most prolific and gorgeous orchid plants imaginable, and poverty and crime that made it a unique experience for second-generation Norwegian immigrants from the Midwest.

By the time I graduated from college I had attended 18 schools in three countries. Perhaps it was from my seafaring Viking ancestors, but somewhere in all this I found that I enjoyed the adventuresome life. In the process I also developed an insatiable desire to see the world. Thus it seemed natural to opt for those opportunities that would take me places. And in those places I have met a lot of fascinating people, had some interesting experiences and learned a lot of lessons.

Two decades after my first trip to South America, I again returned to that continent. Yet when the DC-3 landed on the grassy runway of a small interior town in south Brazil, I had no idea what adventures were in store for me during the next 15 years I was going to spend there. Umuarama, where we landed, was a burgeoning frontier town with wooden sidewalks that kept you slightly out of the mud in a brand-new jungle area which the government then was trying to encourage settlers to open up. Strings of roads went out from towns like Umuarama as pioneers fanned out to cut down the incredible tropical rain forests to plant corn and rice and coffee. There were no paved roads, electricity or telephones. When we drove to Umuarama monthly to buy groceries, someone would sit in the back of the jeep pickup hacking at the trailing vines that constantly tried to retake their invaded territory.

Today Umuarama is a modern little city with microwave telephone communication to the whole world and television sets behind most front doors. The airstrip still isn't paved, but the frontier days were over when an asphalt highway finally reached Umuarama's gate, supplanting that dusty and long twelve-hour ride that used to get us out to civilization and the big lights.

I went to Brazil as a young bride, a year out of college, to help my parents in their mission work there. My husband was to manage a mission farm 35 miles outside Umuarama, down one of those remote jungle trails, and I was to teach school to missionary children. Since well-laid plans tend to change, some nine months after arriving—and two days after my 24th birthday—I found myself the mother of eight Brazilian orphans who had come under the care of the mission. No one knew quite what to do with these children who stairstepped from being almost-two to nine years of age, so we volunteered to adopt them. The next 14 years were busy ones for me as I raised these eight plus two of my own. But that really is a separate story.

At first I was too busy to teach, and by the time my household was organized enough for me to have some time left over so I could do something other than cook, launder, sew clothes and shop, my services as a teacher were no longer needed. Almost accidentally I began writing for magazines and journals. Brazil was an exciting place to be and I had always dreamt of being a writer. Then with my penchant for traveling I was glad to accept assignments that let me travel around South America and attend conferences as far away as Switzerland.

When my Brazilian children were virtually grown, it was time to take my own two, then ten and eleven, out of the jungles so that they could get some "proper" schooling. I headed north, back to California where I had established some roots, and soon found myself the associate editor of *Missiology* which is an academic quarterly journal devoted to the science of mission. Since mission conferences tend to be in exotic places, I again found myself doing what I liked—traveling and writing.

Moving back to the States, I thought meant returning home to the land of my birth/education/culture. Yet I felt foreign to so much that looked familiar. That led me to musings about our American dream castle that not only seemed to be crumbling around me, but also was putting me into culture shock.

Fortunately that first spring a friend's remote desert cabin was made available to me—no running water or electricity or American accoutrements of a basic operating procedure—but it comfortably reminded me of home in Brazil. There in the desert my soul had a chance to make a transition to this noisy, whirling American world of split-second scheduling, frantic freeways and sensory overload. There I retreated to spend nearly every weekend watching the desert flowers blaze into bloom, the sparkling spring gush forth winter rains, feeling guilty about even taking a walk, for every step crushed one of those minute, hardy desert flowers that make you wonder who God had in mind when he created them. Or maybe he was hoping we would kneel a lot?

It had been a winter of unequaled rain and the desert came alive with unequaled glory. C. S. Lewis says that our perception of beauty is one of the surest explanations for the existence of God. I know I felt his presence there in that tiny cabin and felt sad when the spring trickled to dry and the inevitable progression of the summer's heat signaled that my Desert Fox days were over.

But I appreciated the opportunity I had been given to reflect on my life. I was struck by the fact that my Third World experience had been rich in learning and insights I needed to articulate. That desert hideaway eased my adaptation back to the American life-style, and during those quiet weekends when I would muse about my cross-cultural experiences, I became convinced that no matter how at home I would become in North America, I could never leave behind my Latin American background. I was firmly linked to both cultures—belonging to both, responsible to both.

Subsequently in my travels, I realized that as the world is getting smaller, it is easier to see how links exist for us to virtually all our planet's cultures. Then if we are serious about our Christianity, we must admit an ethical responsibility not only to those with whom we are linked together in personal community, but also to those of the world community to whom we are linked by many invisible strands.

Too, I have found in my travels that decisions made here in Pasadena can affect the lives of refugees in the camp of Nong Chan on Thailand's border and the dwellers of Rocinha—Rio de Janeiro's largest shantytown. Their lives and ours have common roots, so if our Christianity demands that we bear each other's burdens, then it is vital that we understand how our life-style and our decisions affect the entire world. Only then will we adequately comprehend our responsibility to our neighbors around the world. As Christians we must know the answer to the question asked of Jesus, "Who are our neighbors?" We must be prepared to emulate the Good Samaritan whenever we happen on any who are fallen by life's wayside.

This book then is a composite of some of the lessons I have learned in my journeys about how people in different cultures cope with life's problems. In observing firsthand how some people who live in what I would call hostile environments survive joyfully, I have come to appreciate value systems that are completely foreign to mine. I have gained much personally from my opportunities to meet these people from diverse communities.

Here and there I have shared these stories with readers and audiences. It seemed timely to organize them and share them more widely. All the stories are true. Sometimes names and places have been disguised when the protection of privacy is necessary—for apparent reasons. The reflections are mine only in that I have them inside, but I know that they have been generated from hours of conversations—on porches, in tree houses or on the beach—with many people whose orbits have intersected with mine and who shared with me their dreams and ideas and reflections. I would be happy to hear your reaction to these musings.

Faith Annette Sand
P. O. Box 60008
Pasadena, California 91106

Chapter _____ 1

Spain and Cultural Trade-offs

Every time you think of some trips, your soul smiles and happy scenes flit by on that videotape recorder you carry around inside your head. My sabbatical in Spain was like that–and Spain turned out to be everything I'd dreamed of–sand-colored castles and whitewashed windmills guarding their memories of Don Quixote and El Cid behind placid fronts. The villages with narrow, winding streets and overhanging verandas could only have been planned by Minos. And it was true. Storks did nest atop every hamlet church, their huge bodies profiled on ancient, vary-hued tile roofs bleached by generations of strong sunlight. I was enthralled by my leisurely meandering through the back roads of this lovely country.

It had been five years since my first trip to Spain–one of those two-day touristy visits–when I had been overwhelmed by how friendly everyone was and how attractive this made the country appear. Franco had still been alive on that trip and from all the bad press he'd gotten, I had come to Spain, expecting to find an impoverished, backwards country filled with sullen peasant types.

Instead, I began to be fascinated by those "sullen peasant types" I began meeting. Driving south from France, I came into the country over a pass in the Pyrenees on a twisty mountain road, guidebook in hand. Suddenly, up close, I came upon a real, live shepherd, his sheep flocked behind him, maneuvering them across the highway with amazing and expert control. Not too sullen-looking, and somewhere I felt a twinge of longing for a world I'd never know, seeing this man against the horizon, alone with his dog and the sheep, as far away from the sidewalk jungle as he could get. Didn't he know that there was an automated world out there to conquer?

That guidebook said a village bar on a Sunday night was an experience not to be missed. Fortunately my two days came on a weekend and I ventured forth to see for myself. It was rather unbelievable–the entire family was obviously there. Men were congregated at the bar with their *chatos* (small glasses of wine), eating *pellizcos* (pinches of fish, squid, prawns or what-have-you), talking of crops, hunting and soccer games; the women sipped tea at the tables gossiping about what only women can gossip about; children were tearing around playing tag while grandfathers, seated in front of the corner TV, were bouncing toddlers on their knees. The young folk were self-consciously milling at the door and stared for a few seconds when I walked in, but soon the happy party continued on–life was too full to stop for a stranger who had no permanent role to fill in their lives.

These people belonged *together*! I was enchanted by the warmth of their community, and further amazed when that warmth reached out to touch me. Driving across Spain, on my way from France to Portugal, I asked directions more than once, and each time total strangers went out of their way to show me where to go. What was with these people? I couldn't quite imagine a Californian driving a half block, let alone a half mile, to show me how to get to a freeway entrance! Yet this happened in Madrid when I couldn't locate the road to Lisbon. By the time I was approaching the border into Portugal, I had completely revised my attitude towards the Spanish people, and knew that if ever I had a chance, I would return and try to understand where all the warmth and love and good vibrations came from.

So it was easy–when I felt the need to get away from my hectic household and take time out to make some serious decisions about my future–to accept the invitation of some new friends who lived in

Madrid to come back and stay in Spain for a half year. My two youngest, Heidi and Heather, then in the fifth and sixth grades, accompanied me on my sabbatical in order to enroll in a real school for the first time in their young careers. We picked an English school where they wore proper uniforms and had to sit at desks—a far cry from their casual jungle classroom. During the week I, too, attended classes at the University of Madrid, but on weekends the three of us wandered the countryside in a little Renault I bought.

It has been my experience that in God's economy, we reap what we sow. Sometimes we think we're planting good seed, but then when we start to harvest, we find we have produced a horrible crop and if we're wise we'll reexamine the seed. This six-month sabbatical gave me an opportunity to reflect on the Spanish culture and see what kind of seeds they had been planting, which became obvious from what they were harvesting.

Every culture in the world has priorities. Some things are more important to one than to another. If two values are mutually exclusive, than according to the priorities, one value is sacrificed and a cultural trade-off occurs. In order to educate my children, I give up a freedom (which I value) to control all my income and pay taxes which support the schools. I also relinquish my children's freedom to control their own time and submit them to a system which says they are delinquent if they are not attending school properly. The trade-off for the loss of these freedoms is consistent with my priority to have well-educated offspring.

One of the great boons to me from my travel around the world is that it has afforded me the opportunity to observe what different cultures are willing to trade off. From these observations I have learned to reevaluate my own trade-offs and ask whether they are worth it. These cross-cultural observations have even made me decide that some of my cultural trade-offs are no longer palatable or even satisfying my needs.

During this sojourn in Spain my impression of the Spanish people kept improving—except for one thing that was infuriating me. I felt stupid about discussing this with the Spaniards with whom we lived, but finally over tea with an American friend I burst out, "Really, Julia! It's a complete invasion of privacy."

My anger had been roused by the "disgusting" habit of Spanish men who felt they had to comment on my personhood as I walked past them on the street. The first time this happened, I just thought it was some weirdo who felt compelled to speak out. But I soon learned that it was habitual—every time you walked anywhere, you were sure to have someone say something to you somewhere along the way. Julia seemed to be the right confidante—the sedate pastor's wife from the English-speaking congregation we had joined; surely she had learned how to cope with this problem during her ten years in Spain.

The last thing I anticipated was to see Julia's eyes twinkle in response to my query. She said, "I can guarantee it, Faith, that if you accept it for what it is—a compliment—you'll miss it after you leave Spain."

Instead of disclosing some Spanish equivalent of the Italian hat pin, here Julia, an enigmatic smile on her sweet, grandmotherly face, was telling me (with my American/Puritanical background) that I should enjoy the whole process and take it as a compliment. I stared at her wondering just how much the church had been compromised here in Spain.

Julia read my incredulity, so went on to illustrate with a story about her daughter Susan's trip to England several years before when all those miniskirts were such a rage over there. Susan came back to conservative Spain's longer skirts saying, "Do you know, Mom, why all those English girls wear their skirts so short? Those guys don't even know girls exist! Not one boy said a single thing to me the entire trip. Those girls dress that way to try to get attention."

We laughed at Susan's culture shock on returning to our Anglo milieu, but by the time I had finished my tea, I somehow had become a bit more tolerant person. After that I took Julia's advice to the extent that I stopped giving angry glares to all those invaders of my privacy and tried to ignore the *guapa*, *rubia* and other comments which were much too sophisticated for my Spanish to compute.

And even that intrigued me—I look too Nordic to ever pass for an Iberian. Most people in Spain immediately assumed I was one more of the million Scandinavian tourists that visit their country annually. So those comments were obviously being made with no intent of what Americans call communication at a meaningful level. These men had to be saying something to themselves which was important enough to bother. But what was it?

I started to observe the Spanish women and became fascinated with how they responded to these sidewalk commentators. They never reacted in any observable way, yet it was there. Somehow those women managed to walk, heads held high, while still giving off a light feeling of, "I'm hearing you. I appreciate what you're saying. It has added to my day." Yet all done aloofly and with no visible response.

Later when I left Spain, I realized that Julia had been right. Though it was difficult to admit, I did miss the aura of Spanish life that made me feel more of a woman and would give me pause in the morning to dress with a little more care for that audience out there that awaited me. Maybe that explains why most little girls still wear skirts in Spain–even when they're playing hopscotch or roller skating down the sidewalks.

Heidi and Heather never did manage to get acculturated in that respect. My Spanish friends and I would laugh at how they and their American playmates would stand out of any Spanish crowd of children. It wasn't only their short, blond hair and casual jeans that set them apart, even when they would go off to school in their proper English uniforms–kilts, white shirts, jumpers, knee-high socks and sturdy shoes–they still managed to come home looking American–their shirt tails hanging out, socks fallen to the ankles exposing the perennially scabbed knee, looking slightly askew. Their Spanish playmates, on the other hand, would look completely kempt even after an hour of wild rope jumping with the girls! I would compare them to my rumpled progeny, but never figured out their secret. How had the art of play dresses been lost to us?

In Spain women wear dresses all the time–for going to market, picnicking in the park, staying home with the children. Somehow it becomes important to appear very feminine. Then I began to wonder what connection this had to the absence of what I considered to be a women's lib movement in Spain. American women living there tend to get angry when their husbands must sign official papers for them to borrow money at a bank or open a business. Mention this to a Spanish woman and the look is definitely haughty, as if to say, "Why bother hassling such a trifle?" Another attitude hard for me to compute.

There was other data complicating my printout: Why is Spain one of the safest countries for a woman alone to travel? at any hour of the day or night? Why is there relatively little street crime?

I had my own culture shock when I returned to my native land. It had been several years since I'd been to New York and it gave me pause to find cab drivers taxiing about in what amounted to armored vehicles, protecting themselves from their clients. Who were the people everyone feared so? Was I vulnerable too?

It was also distressing later to settle into a California community whose streets are deserted the moment the sun goes down. The local stores sell whistles which the Rotary Club advises the elderly to wear at all times to help prevent crime. I put this into juxtaposition with Madrid's streets where there are as many strollers downtown at midnight as there are in Los Angeles at noon.

Moving to the U.S. meant that I had to modify my habits drastically from what had become comfortable in Spain. In Madrid I had traveled three nights a week by subway across the city to get to my classes at the university. (When I started doing this, I had asked Spanish friends if it was safe to do so. They laughed and assured me there would be no problem. And there never was. I had nary a scary incident–but couldn't help later comparing this experience to the New York subways!)

Back in the States my relatives and friends repeatedly asked how it felt to return to the best country in the world. What struck me was that if I ever mentioned the possibility that there are other places in the world where the living is great, I felt as though I was being un-American. There were certainly some questions in my mind about our best American society when it came to personal safety. Yet it seemed to threaten my friends if I pointed this out.

Then to use my rule of thumb, I started looking at the seed we were sowing in our society that made us reap the violence and the street crime. What cultural trade-offs had we made that the Spanish weren't making?

In California I dropped in on a childhood friend, Paula, who is now a psychologist. Knowing my penchants, she immediately put the teakettle on the stove and we started catching up on our different happenings. When I got to my time in Spain I began going over my still-hazy impressions until one response she made started to bring the picture more into focus. Paula said that psychological studies are showing that alienation, loneliness and low self-esteem are characteristics of the Western technological culture.

Quite some trade-offs for all our cars and superhighways and efficient chrome kitchens.

But it was so true. I flipped back to my observations during the 18 years I'd lived in Latin America. At first it had been hard for me to understand people who were not goal oriented. I had pitied their stupidity and how deprived they were of modern technology. But slowly I began to wonder just who was stupid. Especially in the

Brazilian interior where there was no electricity and no TV, the people I knew had such a calm life-style that they had space each day to sit on the porch and watch the breathtaking colors be painted across the sunsetting sky—an incredible substitute for the most advanced colored TV.

These neighbors of mine could also play with their children for hours and thought nothing of walking with friends for 12 miles to the store and back. They lived in a family-oriented culture which kept even the most ancient or infirm from being excluded from the circle. Everyone fulfilled an important role within the community and they felt good enough about themselves so they didn't consider it wasting time to enjoy the sunset instead of rushing off to meet another goal to add meaning to life.

When I first thought about the differences between my Brazilian counterparts and myself, I resolved my perplexities by deciding we just danced to different tunes, meeting different individual needs. Talking with Paula I began to wonder how much a goal-oriented life-style is actually the result of a low self-esteem, so that with every goal we set and reach, we hope to feel better about ourselves. I know if I felt good enough about myself I wouldn't be taking classes all the time.

Reflecting on my stay in Spain seemed to confirm these ideas. Several times during those months Heather, Heidi and I had visited friends in the Basque area. Their home in the Navarrian village of Olite is estimated to be 700 years old and they were the direct descendants of the first owners, for all anyone knew. The bottom floor consists of an entryway and a horse stall cum horse; the living quarters are on the second and third floors. From the roof you can see the spires of the local medieval castle—one of the most beautiful in all Spain I decided after concentrated castle hopping.

You can drive through the walls that still surround Olite and get to their home on one of those twisting, narrow cobbled streets, but when two cars meet, one backs up around the corner to let the other one by. The town was always a unsolvable labyrinth to me, but their first day there Heather and Heidi skated their way to comfortable familiarity. From then on they thought it hilarious that they had to guide my groping path through town.

Our friends, Julio and Abilena, made their living (with the help of that horse downstairs) from six acres of land—in three inherited parcels. It was incomprehensible to them that we lived on a 5,000 acre mission farm in Brazil. That year Julio had 30,000 liters of wine in the local co-op waiting to be sold.

But what impressed me most about Julio and Abilena wasn't their ability to make a good living from what seemed to my Brazilian-trained eyes to be a handkerchief-sized farm, but rather their complete lack of having to upgrade or do anything. This family didn't need to buy a plusher car, to add on a tennis court or to make a world cruise. I was the first Protestant they'd ever spoken to. They were interested in where I'd been and what I'd done, but somehow I knew there was no envy in this interest. In fact I felt there was a twinge of pity from them because I had not had the privilege of being born in Olite—the best spot on God's green earth.

Basically, Abilena and Julio simply did not want. They were satisfied. They knew where they had come from and were content to be going exactly where their parents had gone. In the prosperity of that good wine year they decided to give a bit more to the church, but the life-style their families had maintained in this village for generations was good enough for them.

On my first visit to Spain I had changed my mind about Franco, recognizing his reasons for keeping 20th century technology, with its inherent greed structure, at bay in an effort to maintain the good life. It was a cultural trade-off he had not wanted to make, and he had had the strength to make it happen. I didn't know about the ethics of his government, but I could understand his motivation. And that visit had strangely made me more accepting of the Latin American life-style where I lived.

My second trip to Spain convinced me that they were reaping some good crops from seed which our culture had forgotten to plant somewhere along the way. It still wasn't clear exactly what that seed was, but I wanted to delve into the issue.

Paula didn't know that while she was getting our tea things organized, what she had said had mentally taken me to Spain and back. She listened to my tales and started musing with me about the different seeds planted by the two cultures. Did I know that the latest American sociological findings indicate that crime is not linked to poverty, as had been assumed, but rather to a breakdown of family structure?

The picture was getting clearer: Spain, with its strong family structure and emphasis on tradition, had little street crime. The price of upward mobility and a technology-oriented society was too high for them. In the same vein, women's lib is not an issue because women in Spain aren't required to be men. They enjoy being women because men enjoy being men.

In our culture where it is so important to upgrade and progress and make a better life for ourselves than our parents were able to give us, it is almost imperative that the wife/mother enter the work force. And if she is there, then it is fair that she be paid at the same level men are–which unfortunately the statistics prove just is not happening.

If upward mobility weren't the issue, most women would not have to lead the frenetic lives they now do. And of course it is fair, if both husband and wife work outside the home, that they share equally in the child raising and the house responsibilities. The women's lib movement is, after all, a justice issue. It is as wrong to exploit women and pay them at an inferior rate for equal jobs as it is to exploit slaves. Women in America are angry because they really are being victimized by an unjust system.

In Spain the set roles for the men and the women give a stability, a permanence and a security which are the counterparts of alienation, low self-esteem and loneliness. Women aren't angry, because they don't feel exploited.

I am a very independent woman and appreciate that women in America now have choices and options we never had before–I think. Also I know it is impossible to turn back the clocks. Having made decisions and ushered in a new age, we can never go back to a discarded life-style, because the new choice will always be informed by the new experience.

On the other hand it is the frustrated people of this world who move in new directions and accomplish new things. The happy ones are content to sit at home on their front porch swings enjoying. At the back of my mind I've known that a white picket fence around a cottage that would always be there, a couple kids, and a calm and simple life would have provided me with a completely fulfilling life. I never did get that and have subsequently been seen as a goal-oriented producer.

But it was out of this production that I began to build resentments. I could never understand why, for doing the same work that males do, I was not getting the same recognition, the same power or the same money. Worse than being underpaid, it seemed that any success that I achieved became a threat to the male-types in my life.

Even here Paula had something to say: Interestingly enough, people in the field of psychology were finding that the women's lib movement in America wasn't affecting females as much as it was males who no longer knew their roles in life. Their insecurity seemed to be linked to an identity crisis–they didn't know who they were any more or what role they were supposed to fill. Yet in most cases they had sown the seeds that caused these cultural changes they found uncomfortable. They wanted a better life or someone to put them through school, which brought women into the marketplace, but then didn't know what to do with these competent women who were in the marketplace.

Consequently I've been glad for this experience in Spain where I began to see that our family roles and our family ties could well be reevaluated. We would do well to learn from the Spaniards how to cherish these family roles a bit more vigorously. After all, role playing isn't all bad. It doesn't detract from my independence to allow some man to open a door for me or show me some courtesy that makes me feel feminine. Nor does it make me a lesser person to know I have better culinary skills than most men I meet. Cleaning kitchens tends to be a drag, but changing my car's oil definitely seems draggier. It's a trade-off I'm willing to make. I've wired lamps, drilled holes in my plaster wall for toggle bolts that hold up kitchen shelves installed by yours truly, but the end conclusion remains: I don't *need* a man around to do such chores, but I don't *need* to do them to feel good about myself.

Perhaps the time has come for us to look closely at our cultural trade-offs. Is more wealth, more power, more of anything worth the harvest we've been reaping lately? I think we should consider the trade-offs we've been making for our freedoms–freedom to be lonely and alienated and have a low self-esteem. It ends up a high price.

We can't go back to a rural or village life, but we can opt for a simpler life with less technology and a slower pace, thus mitigating the demands made on us by the computerized numbers system. We can stop wanting and start enjoying what we have.

I left Spain pining to some extent for their life-style, wishing that as Americans we were able to recapture a bit of what they had. Of course we can't become Spaniards, but we can let our cultural trade-offs be informed by the Spanish cultural trade-offs, and we can examine ours to see if they're really worth the prices we are paying for them.

Leaving Spain, I also knew I would like to retire there someday, because it isn't a sin in Spain to grow old. They are horror-struck to hear about our old people's homes where we shunt the nonproducers in our society. When production is your main criterion, it becomes understandable that you try to eliminate the drags on production from the mainstream of society. But when enjoyment is your prime motivator, old people aren't an anathema.

Old people can even be perceived as beautiful. It seemed appropriate that on my last day in Spain, as I was waiting on the corner to hail a taxi, I saw a nicely-dressed woman, well past her prime, coming down the sidewalk. Just then an elderly, gray-haired gentleman rounded the corner, saw her, and made an appropriate– I'm sure–comment on her personhood. Not a lash flickered. But I was happier for having seen this stroking incident.

I decided then that when my wrinkles are prominent and I'm no longer making meaningful, productive contributions to my society, this is the culture where I want to be. Even though I still don't understand why these Spanish men need to admire the fleeting woman as she passes by, I have decided that probably it would be something I'd appreciate in my dotage.

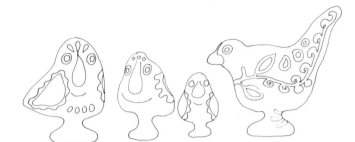

Chapter _____ 2

From Brazil to Snowflakes

The trip I almost turned back from was the one that moved me to Brazil at age 23. At first I thought it was going to be rather adventuresome—along with my newly-acquired husband, I had eagerly bundled up the accoutrements of our world plus Twinkie, our Siamese cat, and Ginger, our cocker spaniel dog. But by the time I was headed for the plane, I was not only slightly frazzled, but also just plain scared. I was starting an odyssey to the jungles of southwest Brazil where my parents had been missionaries for several years.

Whatever adventuresome spirit I might have possessed, ebbed to zero when I was handed my boarding pass and started to say good-bye to the many friends who had come to the airport to see us off on our jungle adventure. Suddenly, tears streaming down my face, I was besieged with fears and doubts about the wisdom of abandoning our very comfortable world to go to a remote mission farm!

I felt somewhat better some five days later when the last of the planes we boarded, a DC-3, came rolling to a gentle stop on the grassy runway in Umuarama, Parana, Brazil, and I spotted my mother waiting alongside the jeeps and pickups and people who clustered at the end of the runway. There was no terminal, so the plane had buzzed the town, and anyone expecting to meet some-one on the plane rushed out to the airport, forming the official welcoming committee. There were no telephones in town, but you could radio ahead and tell people you were coming.

Umuarama is Guarani Indian for "where friends meet". I didn't know that then, but I did know the people I met were gracious and warm and that we were going to be friends. My fears began to sub-side and I knew we had made the right decision in coming—even though there were plenty of surprises ahead of me!

We landed about noon. What with one thing and another (the one thing being a most amazing 50-cent T-bone steak lunch, the another being a tropical rainstorm which stuck a big truck right in the middle of the one-lane road with jungles on either side so our smaller pickup had to make a very long detour) we got home after seven.

To my city eyes my parents' house looked like something out of a rustic summer camp. There were kerosene lights, kerosene refrigerators (I never knew they even existed!) and battery-run shortwave radios. All in all a most primitive existence, I decided in the first glance around the unpainted, unvarnished wood house with homemade furniture—a table, some chairs, a single bed that was pillowed into looking like a sofa. "How come you're still camp-ing out?" I asked.

My folks had been on this mission farm for three years and it seemed time enough to make it part of the 20th century. I didn't know then the sheer energy that was needed just to survive in those jungles, which left little time to devote to the efforts required in trying to accumulate the comforts I had become used to having in the States, nor did I realize how frugally everyone lived on that mission station.

Technically we were in what was called semitropical rain forest (we were 16 miles south of the Tropic of Capricorn and 35 miles east of the Paraguay border), on the true Brazil frontier. But rather untechnically, Twinkie, on that first evening, at long last out of her traveling cage, ran outside and within her first ten minutes of Brazilian freedom killed a very small black snake. I instantly surmised that a bigger snake would have easily carried Twinkie off to its lair and eaten her. I also instantly surmised that there were a lot of adjustments I was going to have to make to live happily-ever-after here.

To me it was a raw jungle that never became a comfortable spot of this world to settle in. Seeing a huge spider today— some 20 years later— still puts me into orbit. The family joke is that you can tell the size of the spider by the decibels of my scream. I have tried not to scream— but my Nordic blood genetically prepared me to brave cold seas, privations and long winters— not humid jungle living. Coping with the long summer heat exhausted six months of every year.

Yet I found myself enchanted by Brazil, the guileless frontier people who came to find their fortunes much as my migrating ancestors had gone to America in quest of theirs. I learned their language and then began to learn and appreciate the Brazilian way of life. It was so different from the one I'd left in the States. There I had schizophrenically divided my time between a staid, tree-lined small college town in the Midwest and a Southern California mega-lopolis with scurrying freeways and tall palms swaying over sunny towns which valiantly ignored the fact that they were really a desert-made-oasis thanks to the rerouted Colorado River.

But the jungle climate and new language were easier to adapt to than the weird mores that I soon realized existed there. I found it hard to appreciate the Brazilian culture which says that people are more important than programs. Whizzing my way through school and jobs in America, I had always vied for the top slot— the best grade, the highest position, the most organized program. After 20 years of being carefully taught how to produce, I was dropped into a culture whose values were literally foreign to mine. And I found this most frustrating.

When people are more important than programs it means that your carefully planned life becomes filled with emergencies. Even such simple things as inviting friends to come to dinner! Of course the difficulties were compounded by not having telephones, for you never knew just what to expect.

Should friends drop in on your expected guests just as they were preparing to come your way, they would have various options: they could stay and entertain their visitors awhile, getting late to your house so that the souffle would have long ago sunk to the bottom of the dish; they could bring the new visitors along so you would have to graciously smile as you squeezed more plates and silverware onto the loaded table; or if the visitors' needs were deemed more important than keeping this social commitment, your friends would apologize effusively the next time they saw you.

Waiting for the no-shows almost gave me ulcers which were only compounded by finally eating—cold food, too late, too fast.

But time taught me that there were some good sides to this Brazilian bias, and I came to value the beauty of a system that can always *dar um jeito*. This is a great, untranslatable term in Portuguese which literally means "make a way". And it is one of the most common expressions used. Whenever a program or policy or system becomes an obstacle to a personal need, someone is sought who can *dar um jeito*. Thus should you come up against some difficulty, some regulation or some red tape that doesn't allow you to do something you need/want/are obligated to do, there is always someone who will take pity on your personhood to *dar um jeito*. When you have an insurmountable problem, you become the suppliant asking those around to *dar um jeito*—make the impossible possible.

Of course one of the ways employment levels are kept up in Brazil is that there are a lot of people involved in braiding a complicated red tape system. But this also gives employment to others whose speciality becomes unbraiding those plaits. These are the people expert in finding out how to *dar um jeito* to get you an absolutely essential document which takes a minimum of a week, but which you need tonight so you can attend a funeral tomorrow in Houston. It's a warm fuzzy feeling you get as you sit on the plane that evening knowing someone out there in red tape land cared enough about your personal tragedy to *dar um jeito*.

Newly-arrived Americans in Brazil rant and rave a lot about the inefficiency of it all and how one good computer would solve the whole problem, but I've never heard of a computer giving out warm fuzzies, and something is lost when we only speak to each other in binary FORTRAN.

After 15 years of living in the jungle of Brazil, learning to accept their systems and adjust to the Brazilian ways (but never the climate!), I moved back to the U.S., bringing Heather and Heidi with me. And strangely enough one of the hardest things for me to do was to adapt myself back to a culture that said programs and policies were more important than people. No one here was interested to *dar um jeito*. Regulations were set in concrete, and that was final.

Back in America I found myself missing that Brazilian charm that drove so many American friends crazy. Of course one reason no one had to *dar um jeito* was that life was incredibly organized. This was evident from all the efficiency/technology/tight-time schedules that worked.

In spite of how nice it was not to have to bribe every official in town to get a driver's license, I still began to appreciate the Brazilian culture in a new way, and realized that in many ways I had become Brazilian on the inside. I reacted to the harshness of the American programs that made people into objects with numbers tattooed on their brains. To *dar um jeito* would be to upset the system, make the efficient swampy, the crystal-clear murky, but in the end it would be a lot more human.

The adjustments I had to make back to America were nothing compared to that of my jungle babies, Heather and Heidi, now eleven and twelve. When I had first brought them out of the jungles it had been a grand adventure exploring a new world through their eyes. At times it was a bit embarrassing to have to hush them when they enthusiastically (and loudly) pointed out the marvels of an escalator or an automatic door. Strangers would turn and stare at us wondering under what bush I had isolated these normal-appearing children so that they would exclaim over such commonplaces.

Forever gone for them were those days of casual studying habits when they did their correspondence courses on the porch, overlooking the wide panorama of the valley that stretched away from our home, allowing themselves to be distracted by every passing butterfly. Now they had to submit to a regimented system behind secluded walls where bells and obligations ruled their lives. They appreciated the incredible advantages of being back in the world of electricity and telephones and the ubiquitous television, but in their attempt to adjust to this American world, the question that kept being asked was, Which system was better—the American's or the Brazilian's?

There was no easy answer. The girls were evaluating amazing new sights. But even I, though looking at very familiar scenes, was filtering these scenes through 15 years of jungle experience, so my perceptions were changed. What I had taken for granted two decades before, I questioned now. A self-service gas station didn't seem to be an efficient way to save money, but a ridiculous way to take jobs away from kids who needed them while getting me grubby and crabby in the process of filling my gas tank—a trade-off I thought was stupid.

I was glad enough to leave behind the spiders, biting insects and heat which had plagued me for years, but the life in Brazil had idyllic qualities that we all mourned, which made some American systems appear inferior to us. I found that I had developed a very different world view from my relatives and friends, and I was going through as much culture shock as I had when I first moved to Brazil.

Though outwardly it seemed I quickly adjusted to the American scheme— after all, my roots were used to that ground— I no longer thought of the American Way of Life as being superior to that of the rest of the world. Just different. We were just making those cultural trade-offs that some parts of the world found unpalatable. And as I had once thought American visitors didn't understand and tended to be unnecessarily critical of Brazilian systems, now my relatives thought I was being unnecessarily harsh about the American Way of Life which they assured me was the best in the world— my friends Julio and Abilena to the contrary!

A trip to Sequoia National Park in California's High Sierras finally helped bring some clarity to the issue of deciding which system was better. That first year we found ourselves making grand forays into nature. Our souls were being jumbled by all the noises and frenetic activity of the city, so as often as possible we tried to escape to the remoter corners which felt more like our old life in Brazil and where the quiet restored us to peace.

But there were a lot more strictures on us than there had been in Brazil— where the girls' correspondence course could be manipulated to suit our schedules and we were much freer to follow our whims. Now even I was in seminary, so we were all obligated to fall in step. When Thanksgiving holiday finally rolled around, and since snow is still special to us, it took little urging from our good friend Judy to escape to Sequoia National Park with her.

Sequoia isn't one of America's most famous national parks, but I have always loved its majestic and quiet beauty. Not only does it contain a grove of the world's largest living creatures— the giant sequoia trees, some of which are three millennia old— but trails lead to caverns that have housed Indians for generations and out-of-the-way places which afford hikers sweeping vistas of California's Sierra High Country.

There in Sequoia, God's snowflake principle overwhelmed me: The Lord has put a lot of energy into making things different. He has made every snowflake that ever fell to be unique! That principle extrapolates to every other created thing. As we wandered beneath those gigantic trees which were tall before Christ was born, what amazed me was, not only are all snowflakes specially created by God, but there aren't even two rocks that are the same.

As Judy and I thawed before the lodge's large fireplace that afternoon waiting for the girls to get cold enough to come in out of the snow, we began musing together on the snowflake principle and how it applied to our lives. Later as we all muffled our way through the snow to climb Moro Rock, we stood on snow-covered heights that overlooked immense valleys enclosed by some of the highest peaks in America. Judy suddenly stopped, tilted her head and said, "Listen! Even God's silences are different!"

But of course! There is a special kind of wilderness silence when you are down in the valley beside a tumbling, ice-cold river. It listens differently as you stand on snow in a cathedral of redwoods in the warming afternoon and plops of melting snow fall around. At the top of Moro Rock the silence was almost scary with the cold, cutting wind winging its way up from across the far reaches of the valley.

If God had made nature to be a kaleidoscope of silences, rocks and snowflakes so that we are always overwhelmed by its variety, and has even given a special, individualized name to each one of us because he is going to communicate with us on a direct one-to-one basis, why do we spend so much time trying to make everyone the same? And why was I worrying about whether American-style or Brazilian-style was better? God loves diversity so much he has engineered it so that snowflakes are different and people are different. He doesn't want cultures to be homogeneous. And he certainly doesn't speak Esperanto!

My wanting cultures to be the same is like trying to manufacture houseplants out of plastic molds. At first glance they might appear to be almost genuine, but in the factory they sit, row after identical row. Intuitively we know that God had nothing to do with this simple product— his are those marvelously complicated, never-to-be-replicated leaves, snowflakes and rocks. Agreed, snowflakes have certain basic qualities (six-sided, appear white, exist only within a particular temperature range, and the rest), but their exquisite differences are much more startling. God apparently really vibrates on variety. Then why are we so bent on getting everything to look as though it had come out of a tacky, plastic mold?

Instead of worrying about those American visitors in Brazil griping about some Brazilian whatever which was inferior to its American counterpart, I now realized it was merely a matter of perspective. Each culture bring different criteria to judge what is good or bad. Since Americans see efficiency and technical production as top priorities, they will allow virtually nothing to stand in the way of getting the job done. But efficiency happens to be quite low on the Brazilian totem pole of priorities.

My present dilemma emerged from the fact that during my 15 years in Brazil I had come to appreciate Brazilian standards, knowing that their value system worked for them. But the American system also worked. At last my contemplation on the snowflake made me realize that one system didn't have to be judged better than the other just because it was different.

Americans raise their children with a quasi-religion that says, "God helps those who help themselves." But this is a mold that doesn't fit everyone. In fact, I disagree with it and can appreciate why Brazilians certainly don't buy this precept. After all, the mystics and hermits in the desert and the contemplative nuns in their cloisters don't fit into that standard. Since they don't significantly contribute to the GNP, at best Americans will tolerate them, but most often they are seen as not quite normal. Certainly American parents would never point out the religious hermit and mystic as models to their children, yet in some cultures they are considered to be the elite of the society. As difficult as it is for Americans to understand, these nonproducers are the most emulated people of some communities.

I'm not espousing the happy native syndrome, nor am I implying that everything Brazilian is ideal, but I do know that different cultures choose different priorities to meet their own felt needs. We are proud of our America from shore to shore or from the automatic doors at the port of entry to the golden arches through which all must pass to get to that American haven of rest: the retirement community cum golf course, swimming pool, 24 hours of planned activities and security guards. Though this meets the needs of a host of Americans, such a life goal would seem anathema to some cultures.

We can be proud of many things in America, but we shouldn't try to export this American dream to one and all. Nor should we condemn out of hand those cultures which really don't appreciate these American goals. Margaret Mead once said it was wrong to try to sell the American life-style abroad because the world's ecosystem could only support one America. I think God only wanted one.

If he has made every snowflake unique, surely he doesn't have a set life-style pattern for everyone. Not only the Brazilians, but all the world's cultures, have a right to operate with their own standards. It is OK for Brazilians not to have efficiency and production as their primary goals, just as we have the right to hold them dear. Brazilians, and much of the world, prefer to have as their main criteria the relationships around them. Status quo is more important than producing and progressing. It isn't wrong to want to maintain their world with the same standards that prevailed when their grandparents were alive, it just means that they won't be able to have chrome-shiny cars to be thrown on the city dump every couple of years.

Americans who are offered a promotion and a ten percent raise to move their families—leaving behind their roots, their community and their comforts to brave a new suburban frontier, new schools and new clubs—will normally do so. Our mobility rate is among the highest in the world. There are many cultures where the trade-offs inherent in such a move would preclude anyone's being willing to make it.

I had a Brazilian neighbor, Messias, who was offered a new job in the city with a 300 percent raise plus benefits that would normally have turned any rural person's head (i.e., house with electricity, running water, refrigerator and television, jeep with driver, plus all the rice and beans his family could consume during the year!). He turned it down. The improved material goods didn't stack up to an improved life-style for him. Leaving the jungle/frontier meant he would be distancing himself and his family from their relatives and friends and a community where they belonged. His wife Chichi was inconsolable at the thought that she would be able to visit her family only once or twice a year. Their priorities meant that it would be better to live a simpler rural life without many amenities and yet enjoy their life-style more.

In fact, I think many of my American friends who have regularly been moving during the past couple of decades to get better paying jobs or to improve their living surroundings, can appreciate Messias and Chichi's decision to opt for a lower salary, a ruder life that allowed them to hold onto the things they found more important— their family, their roots, their community.

So instead of claiming as Americans to have the best culture in the world— which the rest of the world sees as sheer arrogance— perhaps we should stop and contemplate other cultures to understand why they are equally satisfying to their proponents. And in doing this we would gain some new insights into what God is trying to say through all this diversity.

The strangest thing for many Americans to realize is that God doesn't love us best, and he probably doesn't even think we've got the best country or culture in the world. We might have a high degree of technology available to a wide portion of our population and a lot of prosperity for lots of our people, but for any who read the New Testament, this can also be seen as a curse. The disciples never could understand why Jesus said it was harder for a rich person to get into heaven than for a camel to go through the eye of the needle. But Christ did say this, so maybe God looks on us with pity because our wealth has precluded our ever really having much stature in heaven. Or even being able to hear some important things God would like to say to us here on earth.

Maybe you have to be a widow with a mite or an outcast Samaritan to really understand what God wants from you. It would behoove us when we come into contact with people from other cultures— immigrants, refugees, undocumented laborers— to approach them with humility, wondering what our God who loves diversity has taught them that we still haven't learned.

Since God has put so much energy into making individualistic snowflakes, it probably indicates that he's not too interested in our becoming clones of some ideal, efficient, super-achiever/super-producer model. But rather, since we are all created equal in God's sight, it would indicate our cultures probably are pretty equal too. By being humble and listening to each other, we might be able to reflect on our own culture's weaknesses and learn from others around us.

So not only does my snowflake God love diversity, he has probably allowed a lot of diversity so the lessons one culture learns which get obscured in another can be shared back and forth to the benefit of both. We are all part of a world community and we have responsibilities to one another in this world community. Both Brazil and America have contributed insights to me of God's dealing with us here on this earth. And Sequoia's snowflakes will always remind me of the glorious diversity to be found in God's chef d'oeuvre.

Chapter _____ 3

Sequoia National Park and Links

On that trip to Sequoia Judy and began talking about what I considered one of the worst heresies ever expounded in America, i.e. God helps those who help themselves. The subject was illustrated for us in a resounding way.

One problem with God's creatively made snowflakes is that when they're amassed together, they become difficult, if not dangerous, to drive on. We had gotten to Sequoia in a station wagon which my sister-in-law, Betty, had given me when we had first arrived in the States. It was one of those cars which had been in the family generations— about— and was affectionately called the Blue Bomb by one and all. Some drunk had once sideswiped it and it looked rather battered around the edges, but it was still a member of the family in good standing.

After my 15 years in the jungles, the Blue Bomb was just what I needed. Since in many ways the jungles had been an intellectual wasteland, I had been eager to study and so had enrolled in seminary. I was only working part-time in order to concentrate on my studies

and my writing, so was happy not to have to buy a car to get
around in.

Since the girls and I settled only a few blocks away from both our
schools, our lovable Bomb wasn't put to much test. I knew nothing
about the innards of my movable beast, but a fellow student, Tom,
decided his gift to missions that year was maintaining the Bomb for
us. That suited me just fine. The first time Tom did a tune-up on the
Bomb he came to me with a surprised look on his face to tell me that
it was a great car! (I had already told him that, but somehow he had
paid me little heed!) The motor would carry us for another 10,000
miles, he said, easily. The body . . . well, you can't have everything.

Before leaving for Sequoia, Judy had come by to discuss plans for
our trip. I told her that Tom had assured me that the Bomb would
get us where we had to go. Roomy it was. Also smooth, heavy and
slightly extravagant on gas consumption. It was snowing in the
mountains, Judy informed me, so to get into Sequoia we would
need chains.

I had only dim recollections of some male-types in my world
doing chain-type things to cars traveling in deep snow, but after
moving to a tropical clime, my driving expertise centered mainly
on developing a canny sense of knowing which rut to choose to get
through deep mud holes or long sand pits—an unfortunate ability
developed from being stuck in too many mud holes and sand pits
over the years. I knew that snow driving probably needed the same
learning process, but figured that we would muddle through. Judy
said she could borrow chains from a friend at her church, but that
the chains might be a little small for an older station wagon. Again
we figured we could cope.

The park ranger who patrolled the area with the sign that said,
All cars beyond this point MUST have chains, stood looking at us
with the strangest expression on his face. Judy is a liturgical dancer,
lithe and slim. I am uncomfortable around cars and tend to look out
of my element whenever the hood goes up—it was probably this
quality of mine that made Tom take one look at the Bomb and
decide to become our family mechanic. So when Judy and I stood
in front of this park ranger's gaze trying to figure out how—without
taking off our woolen gloves or getting too grubby in that dirty
snow—we could get those chains on the tires and proceed into the
park, we thought if he had a drop of manly blood, he'd offer to
help.

He made no move to even lean our way, so we decided that
1). the art of chivalry was finally completely dead here on the American frontier, or 2). the ranger was under strict orders not to help
motorists with chains, or 3). he was hoping we would give up and
go away because he could tell we weren't the type to spend a
weekend successfully driving over snowy roads in Sequoia.

Little did he know!

Besides being resourceful women, we had a lot of determination
and basic confidence that the God of our pilgrimages who had
brought us this far was going to help us get through this ordeal.
God knew, better than we did, that we needed this R & R.

With no outside help we finally made the ominous and cold
diagnosis that the snow chains were, as suspected, too short to go
completely around the tire. Judy's friend had given her a demon-
stration sans tire on the carpet in their front room which made Judy
head doctor of this operation, but when it came to being super-
creative in finding alternatives, substituting and making do,
nothing beat my jungle training.

With some rubber strips we found in the chain box, we managed
to tie those too-short chains together, and I thought that by driving
slowly enough we could make it to the gas station we knew was a
few miles up the road. By this time the ranger was looking
downright consternated. Off we went and made it into the station
with a final funny clatter as our jerry-rigged snow chains fell off
with perfect timing!

The girls and Judy began merrily making flying angels in the
snow (getting wet and cold, no doubt, I grumbled to myself), while
I told the attendant our dilemma. With carefree aplomb he said he
thought he could fix us up. Judy was now instructing Heather and
Heidi how to make a snowperson, so I supervised Jeff, our friendly
attendant, as he deftly added to our set some links from a box full of
leftover links to send us on our way. To top it off, Jeff not only
solved our problem but told us there would be no charge—he was
glad to help!

Those snow chain links somehow became rather symbolic to us
and we drove away singing and laughing and knowing deep down
that we had a God who cared about us, surrounded us with
wonderful signs of his presence in nature—like the majesty of the
General Sherman Tree which we had just passed—and linked us
to one another here on earth. We needed the Jeffs of this world to
provide us with links for our tires and God knew that Judy, the girls

and I, with the press of school and our myriad duties, needed time away from the city and the lights, being refreshed by the beauty, the quiet, the cold followed by warming fires.

God also knew about our tight student budgets (penurious might be a better term). To get along we needed one another and so God linked us to Judy's friend who loaned us the chains and to Jeff who made them work and produced for us a calming weekend. That trip left us feeling good about being able to put chains on a tire, and about the providential links that happen in the precise moment of need.

As I have traveled around the world I have seen many marvelous sights, but something that seems even more incredible than the greatest waterfall or the oldest tree or the most spectacular sunset is that God has put us all in community and wants us to be linked to one another.

Bearing one another's burdens is how the Bible puts it. That is a very humbling thing to do, because it means you can help someone else and feel good about this act of mercy, but it also means that you are going to need to be helped by someone else. Which really works out to be just the opposite of that God helps those who help themselves. Rather God helps those who help others. Or better still, God has others help those who help others! God links his children together with the most marvelous choreography. I have often wondered what kind of computer he has going to get it as well organized as he does.

Becoming aware of this choreography, being in step with the Choreographer's plans leaves you linked to one another. This was a lot easier for me to learn, somehow, living in rural Brazil. There were times when in order to survive we had to be helped or we had to help the neighbors around us. One of the sad adjustments I made when I moved back to the States was to realize that I was moving back to an individualistic, lonely crowd who had forgotten how important it was to remain linked to one another. There were few Toms and Jeffs to reach out a helping hand. Even our discards we now no longer give to relatives, friends or neighbors in need—we have garage sales. Money becomes our only motivating criterion.

And so I found I had come back to a fast, impatient society where waiting in lines chafes—everyone wants to be first. When Christ said the first shall be last, he meant it, I'm sure. Granted it is the normal human condition to want to be at the head of the line. James and John wanted to be first. I want to be. But Christ said that it was going to be different in his kingdom, and the superstars weren't going to be the ones we would tend to pick out— they would be the little ones, the meek, the humble, the widows giving their mites.

It is easy to forget that the audience is up there, not out there, and the Choreographer's view isn't distorted, like ours tends to be. So the people at the head of the line, the people who are number one, the winners with the medals, those with the most power, aren't the ones who are going to be given the positions of honor in the Kingdom. Rather they will be the people at the back of the line, the people who know they need to be linked to one another because they are too weak to do it alone.

In my years with the missionary community around the world, I have sorrowed to see wide gulfs spread between church communities as missionaries in country after country are accused of neocolonialism. I have long felt that those restless natives out there had plenty of reason for such charges and if anything had probably been overly patient in allowing Westerners to dominate and dictate church affairs in places where the indigenous people were perfectly capable of running their own show.

I think understanding the importance of links would allay a lot of complaints in our missionary world. If we Western missionaries could grasp God's linking mechanism, instead of feeling as though we had a corner on God's market of truth, and could go out to the world not as front-of-the-line winners with superpower, but rather to learn and be helped as much as we are willing to teach and lend a hand, we would be linked together and could establish a true Christian community where we could all grow together.

This principle doesn't only apply to Bonga-Bonga, Jungletown. It also works in Oak Ridge, Suburbanville. Only God knows the superstars of this dance— and there most likely won't be a direct correlation between them and the leaders of our churches. The superstars are the ones who are more related to that mite-giving widow who I'm sure understood links. She had to help others, because she probably had received a lot of help.

Mother Teresa tells the story about giving a meager portion of rice to a starving Indian family who turned around and shared the little they had received with equally destitute neighbors. They were linked to those people in their desperate need and wanted to share their good fortune. The Catholic theologian Rahner would probably call that family Anonymous Christians for they were truly obeying Christ's mandates whether they knew this or not. It is lamentable that our American world has basically forgotten how to share, how to bear one another's burdens, how to be shoe-leather Christians, as my grandmother called them—letting your faith dictate where your feet will go.

A question that consumes a lot of people in seminary, I've discovered, is determining in rather erudite terminology just how much of the gospel needs to be accepted by people before they could be considered Christian. The question really is, How much like 'us' do people need to become before we allow them to link up with us?

This missionary variation of this question is: Just how much does the convert have to buy into the system? Do we need to have church services in steepled buildings at 11 AM on Sunday to be considered good Christians? How much of the Christian pattern can we try to sell? Must a polygamist abandon the extra spouses? What happens to the abandoned women? etc., etc.

I remember the shock I felt in the early '70s when I first heard some sincere African church leaders call for a formal breaking of the links to the Western church by asking for a moratorium on foreign missionaries and foreign funds to their continent. They were not questioning the validity of their Christian faith, they were only troubled by the Western stranglehold on African Christianity, and were even calling our denominationalism a Western form of tribalism. Finding it impossible to dialogue with Western church leaders, they felt they wanted the option to decide whether polygamy, for instance, was all right for their continent. If it was good enough for Abraham, why should people in multiple marriages not be allowed to join the church in Africa?

And since the Africans weren't denying us the privilege of maintaining our denominations—which they found impossible to justify biblically but were willing to allow us as a cultural tribal format of the West—they merely wanted equal rights to their own cultural and tribal forms of Christianity. Instead of Northern Baptist or Southern Presbyterian churches being established in Uganda or Zimbabwe, they wanted the privilege of developing tribal church forms that would conform to their distinctive cultures.

Finally some Africans felt that only a five-year hiatus on Westernized input would give them the space needed to do this. They didn't disparage the valiant efforts made by the Western missionary community to translate the Bible and bring them the message of Christ's special revelation, but they wanted a breather to develop their unused theological muscles and find their own strengths.

For me this was a rational request, yet many missionaries I know have been intimidated by any questioning of the church forms we have advocated around the world for the past two centuries and simply cannot understand why anyone balks at accepting a particular interpretation of church polity as gospel. It is almost as if we were forgetting that it was Christ's gospel we must concentrate on communicating, not our denominational hierarchy.

It always seemed strange to me in Brazil to have all these various denominations striving to establish enclaves of their own works in new areas, instead of working at being linked together. One missionary friend came back from a brand new town on the raw frontier which was the government was trying to open to settlers in northwest Brazil, reporting that already there were 27 different churches established in this one burgeoning town. This can only be called a further extension of cultural diversities. In Africa and South America where community is more important than building skyscrapers or large, successful denominations, and where people are more important than programs and policies, Christian insights tend to stress the importance of links— something which has been hard for Western missionaries to understand.

There's no need to strive for plastic-molded Christians. Rather we can allow God's creativity to work in the various cultures around the world, forming Christians within these particular cultural patterns. Underneath we know we are linked together, and our diversity makes the dance that much more glorious an affair— yet we have to trust our Choreographer throughout!

This does not mean that we should abandon our denominations, Sunday morning services cum organ music and Gregorian chants— they are vital and important to our culture. But they don't have to be integral to the evangelizing of other cultures. Recently I spent a week in Korea at a theological conference, and was strangely offended when I left that country realizing that although I had heard Bach, Handel and many of the good old hymns of my culture, nary a Korean melody had been used in the various churches and seminaries which I visited. What kind of ecclesiastical domination had been used to make these people, who have a very distinctive musical tradition, appear to be clones of the West when singing the Sevenfold Amen to close their Sunday morning service?

Music, in fact, was one reason the Africans called for this moratorium over a decade ago. Not only had the missionaries there introduced church music that is appropriate to the Northern Atlantic culture—but which is as dissonant to them as their tom-toms or Oriental pentatonic scales are to Western ears—but the missionaries also denied them the right to introduce such music into the church, calling it heathen and sinful. These Westerners insisted that African music forms be abandoned without realizing that of course Africans would be more comfortable using their own music—Christian or not—in their religious expressions.

After all, many of our forms of worship and religion have come from pagan sources—like our Christmas trees, our Easter celebrations and even our cathedrals. We have adapted them to our church calendar and feel very good about continuing to use these, so there is no historical reason that other cultures around the world can't do the same with their various traditional celebrations.

Just as my parents felt that the music my generation listened to was sinful, I find myself feeling equally hostile to the music my children like. Yet I also know that by learning to accept the diversity in our tastes, we are free to concentrate on the links that bind us together. This also works on a worldwide scale as we contemplate our differences. God is the Choreographer that wants us all linked together—appreciating what we can learn from one another when we share and are linked—yet developing the humility it takes to accept from others when we are in need.

We are mutually strengthened, not weakened, when we are linked to others who are quite diverse from ourselves. But we have to be in communication with one another to allow this linkage to occur. Just as it was a sin for the priest in the Good Samaritan tale to walk past the wounded, refusing even to look at the victim at the side of the road, so it is a sin for us to turn our heads from our neighbors—regardless of how little we approve of their politics, philosophy or religion—remaining aloof in our isolationism from their wounds. We are called to be linked to one another, cognizant of one another's needs, benefiting from one another's wisdom.

Jesus chose the Good Samaritan to be our model. The Samaritan wasn't theologically acceptable to the Jews, but he pragmatically did the acceptable act and fulfilled a need the two other religiously acceptable persons did not. I would suspect Judy and I were a lot more capable than Jeff of leading a Bible study or discussing theology in depth, but we needed Jeff. He not only helped us get our snow chains working, but he provided a vehicle to a joy-filled week-end.

When we finally left Sequoia we were grateful to a God who cared about our needs, grateful to Jeff for providing part of those needs, and refreshed to go back to our theological world. A bit more humble than when we had arrived— and yet quite proud of the fact that snow chains would never overwhelm us again!

Chapter _____ 4

Reflections on Jonestown

The first night we were in Sequoia, Judy and I decided that after a turkey-sandwich-filled day (we'd had our Thanksgiving a day early and this was leftover weather already), what with travel, children and snow chain adventure, we needed to tuck those girls into their beds, get something hot to drink and relax before the fireplace in the lodge.

It was good to be quiet, mesmerized by the fire. What makes the settling coals and prancing flames so bewitching? We snuggled down comfortably silent, slightly overawed by the beauty of the day and the happy links and the feeling that God loved us.

But somehow all this was incomprehensible in the face of the evening news: someone had imported a newspaper from nearby Visalia, and there in the lodge as we stomped the snow from our boots and warmed our fingers we had read the shocking story from Guyana. After the inexplicable killing of U.S. Representative Leo Ryan along with a party of news personnel, there were now allegedly 200 Americans who had died in the jungles of Guyana. The National

Guard was on its way. No one was quite clear as to how or why these people had been murdered, even though there was some comment about a threatened mass suicide if anyone tried to take over their jungle stronghold. An additional 700 missing Americans were thought to be hiding in the jungles.

My feet were propped up and toasty warm for the first time all day. Suddenly I burst out, "Judy, I know those jungles! Those Americans aren't hiding!" No way could the fragile jungle ecosystem swallow up 700 bumbling, noisy Americans. Some commentator suggested they had dug bunkers and were waiting out the storm there. Ridiculous! The topsoil in the jungles runs 25 to 150 feet deep—and that's a sandy, loose soil, not at all conducive to digging out viable trenches or hidable tunnels. There must have been some foul play. It was so horrible to think about I wanted my mind to change the subject. Some modern-day Hitler would soon be discovered. No way could we believe that 200 people had committed mass suicide. That would have been too stupid. What could have happened?

The next night we repeated the scenario. We had tramped through the snow to Moro Rock and the day had been replete with marveling at how insignificant we were juxtaposed against these gigantic trees, mountains and valleys. Yet we were strangely comforted because we knew that no matter how ant-like we appeared, we were still incredibly loved by the God who had made all this!

But how could we relate this feeling of being loved by the Creator of this breathtaking universe to the horror of Jonestown? That day's paper carried the aching news that 500 were dead! Bodies were stacked up one on top the other, the National Guard reported, and they had found evidence to substantiate the suicide report. How could such a gruesome story be? How could 500 freedom-loving American people allow themselves to be brainwashed into committing suicide? Surely . . . ? But it was not a mistake: they were dead and the gory pictures told a tale no rationalizing could deny.

As we fire-gazed that night, Judy and I were dumbstruck. Someone had heard the radio report: No on had fled; no one escaped. Everyone in Jonestown had committed suicide together— apparently by willingly drinking cyanide-laced Kool-aid. The late news amended the count: the National Guard had come upon 900 bodies— men, women, children, entire families dead in each other's arms. It was then that Judy and I began to work through brainwashing.

The flames leaped high and suddenly I said, "You know, Judy, in many ways much of our education is brainwashing. Much of child discipline is brainwashing! And this isn't all wrong. It's part of learning how to grow up. But how do you decide which is good and which is bad brainwashing?"

We grappled with the implications: Both disciplining a child and brainwashing use a threatened violence of some kind—physical or emotional—to modify or control behavior. I tell my children, "Wash the dishes now, or else . . ." Most of the time the "or else" is implied. When I tell them to do something, they know that I have the authority to enforce their compliance with that order.

Brainwashing also seems to use some subliminal or obvious form of physical or emotional threat. The popular self-actualization groups are infamous because usually one of the first demands of their program is that they begin to exert some form of physical control over their adherents. Sometimes they put strictures on the bladders of the people attending their seminars—not allowing them to use the bathroom facilities except at the will of the leadership. But all of them try to manipulate their proselytes at some physical level.

We do much the same with our children—diaper training is one of the first ways we socialize our children—or brainwash them into accepting our cultural mores. It is as if this is the first step toward controlling whole persons—making their physical functions part of the command system.

This is a subtle, first-step approach to gaining authority over another person so you can go on to modify the behavior of the victim. Whether such behavior modification is beneficial is another question. There are many Christian and evangelical seminar programs which operate on similar lines of behavior modification. Who decides if this is bad or good? And what is the difference between brainwashing that leads to a Jonestown massacre and the discipline that allows a child to grow up to be a functioning, integrated person in our society?

As I stared into the fire, it came to me: Of course! The basic difference is that as a parent or a teacher I must be motivated by love, by that same love that had been overwhelming us that day as we contemplated the beauties of Sequoia and remembered how we felt God's love and saw his choreography in our world so that his creation harmonizes and his creatures help one another. And the reason I wanted to discipline my children was because I loved them and wanted them to fit harmoniously into this wonderful creation.

In order to be accepted by our society they had to obey the basic mores of our society or be considered outcast or unwanted mavericks. A very small child might be excused for going outside on a hot day and stripping—a societal faux pas—but this becomes inexcusable after a certain age. (At least in America. It's fine if you happen to be a Motilone living in the jungles of Colombia.)

I didn't discipline my children because I despised them or thought them basically inferior to me. I knew their potentiality was equal to mine and hoped that someday they would maturely accept full responsibility for making their own decisions. I disciplined them now in order that they might become integrated and responsible members of their society who one day would become completely self-disciplined—coping with their daily dilemmas, exercising their free will to make good and honorable choices, and of course never being cowed into drinking cyanide-laced Kool-aid or taking anything else that is self-destructive.

The best teachers operate out of this same mode. They don't teach to prove how much smarter they are than their pupils, or try to trick their pupils into putting the wrong answer on their exams. They teach in order to open up new vistas on the world and give their students a new platform from which they can spring to new truths and insights and abilities. A jealous teacher who is afraid some student might become greater or more able is seen as an aberration to the teaching profession. To teach is to help. To be a great teacher is to be a great servant motivated by love.

It's an interesting cycle: I must love my children enough so that I can acculturate them to where they can become independent, free-willed agents, making their own decisions, setting their own course in a society where they can in turn raise their own children in the same manner. But the key to all the steps of this operation remains love. The starting point has to be love, and the goal is being cognizant that the most precious gift we have been given by God is our free will. This one characteristic differentiates us from the rest of the created world.

Dogs, cats, lions and turtles don't have to make ethical decisions because they don't have free will. We do, and it gives us the potentiality to achieve glorious heights—like Mother Teresa—or despicable depths—like Jim Jones. Because our free will is the quality which makes us responsible—and ultimately answerable—for our behavior, our free will is an awesome gift which must be disciplined in its proper use. Thus parenthood is such an important occupation. In love, a parent educates and trains a child until that child is capable of making— and living with the consequences of— its own decisions. It is a liberating love.

There couldn't have been much love in Jim Jones' heart if he would prefer to see his followers dead rather than see them escape his control. He certainly must have appeared to be a very loving, charismatic person in order to have all those hundreds of people follow him, but it was a deformed love. Or perhaps at some point his pride swallowed up whatever love he had so he became motivated by his own ego and fixed his intent on controlling the actions of others— getting them to do his will.

Thus the big difference between brainwashing and disciplining is the starting point— the basic motivation. The foundation for a brainwashing syndrome is pride and the end product is to eclipse that great gift of our free will in order to produce a robot willing to drink cyanide-laced Kool-aid on command.

Problems arise in families when the equation of:

motivating love + discipline = free-willed agent capable of managing one's own life

is replaced by any of the aberrations:

motivating pride + brainwashing = robot.

We all know families where parents continue to control grown offspring. There is something pathetic when this happens because it is evident that the parent is motivated not by love but by pride. And that pride is usually a very selfish pride which is willing to destroy the child rather than give up control. The Jonestown incident is only more horrible than such instances because Jim Jones was able to accomplish on such an immediate, large scale what happens in many families at a much slower rate.

There are children who grow old and either because of guilt trips or misguided filial obedience never become adult persons aware of that precious gift of free will God has given to those created in his own image. Granted it was easier for me, as I was raising ten children, to want them to become independent, making their own decisions. Logistically it would have been impossible for me to become a writer and do my own thing if I had tried simultaneously to keep running their lives as they spread out going their various ways. If I had insisted they stay home, tied to my apron strings, doing my will, ignoring their own proclivities, I would have eventually destroyed them as much as Jim Jones did his followers in Guyana. And I would have destroyed myself in the process. Pride is always self-destructive.

Warming by that Sequoia fire, musing with Judy about life, I began to extrapolate these same principles to the church and realized that pride wreaks the same havoc there, especially in the missionary world I knew so well.

A missionary or an evangelist must be motivated by love, not pride, and the result must be a free-willed agent, not a robot. I could immediately think of so many problems I have seen on the mission field and also here at home in U.S. churches I have known which were caused by some parent-type motivated by pride so that when the child-type tried to exercise free will, flexing wings to go off to some new heights, the parent was so threatened by the loss of control that they actually preferred to destroy the child rather than give it freedom.

Yet scarcely anyone in the church preaches against this kind of pride. Humility as a virtue is seldom talked about. It's as though pride isn't all that bad! I remember being shocked one balmy, spring afternoon shortly after coming back to the U.S., driving off to pick up the girls after school, paying more attention to the flowering trees shading the Pasadena street and the sunlight dancing through the leaves than I was to the car in front of me. Suddenly I found myself squinting at a bumper sticker. My eye had been caught by the familiar IXOYE—Christian fish symbol, but I couldn't believe the accompanying sign which boldly said, *I'm Proud to Be a Christian!*

At the time I remember asking myself, "What did pride have to do with being a Christian?" I had always thought pride was one of the seven deadly sins. Then I began to wonder what this slogan said about our Christian world where a promoter could confidently place these two terms side by side, successfully selling the Christian public this kind of heresy. Why don't we put bumper stickers on our cars that say, *Blessed Are the Meek*? Why do we feel that pride no longer is a sin to be eschewed?

Shortly after this I was assigned a popular Christian book to read for a class on church growth. It sought to justify why American preachers needed to be proud. This author felt it was a necessary virtue if they were to have the personal magnetism needed to attract and run multi-thousand congregations. My mind tripped on how this could be added to the beatitudes: "Blessed are the proud... for they shall have huge, successful churches!"

But my questions remained unanswered: In all this, where's the humility and the love and the servanthood that Christ said were to be the cardinal virtues for his disciples? What has allowed us to exchange pride for humility, power and control for love?

And could this be merely a more benign form of mass brainwashing? Could this control by these charismatic leaders in our Christian churches be just another road to slow death?

Of course it is more comfortable for the people in our churches to be told by their ministers and the leaders at the top of the pyramid how to think and pray and make their decisions. But this is very destructive because it stops the offspring from understanding and appreciating the greatest gift God has given to humankind: our ability to choose and to exercise our free will to make ethical decisions and flex those spiritual muscles so that understanding justice becomes an incarnated truth lived out in our own pilgrimages. Becoming robots precludes strengthening this God-given talent, however much more secure it might feel to allow someone else make our ethical decisions for us. It's much easier to have someone else responsible for our actions—but it doesn't make the cyanide-laced Kool-aid any safer to drink.

Later, when I was talking these things over with Paula, my "shrink" friend, she observed that after the Korean War our American psychologists began to study brainwashing in order to discover why our physically powerful fighting Americans turned out to be emotional washouts incapable of withstanding Oriental brainwashing techniques.

Paula said psychologists have categorized our response to stimuli into four areas—by thoughts, by words, by feelings and by actions. That means when someone tells me something, I react by feeling something, by thinking something, by saying something and/or by doing something in response to what has been said. But she also said that what began to surprise the psychologists was the realization, after Korea, that people are not consistent across those four categories, although within the separate categories they tend to be.

That means that my words usually agree with what I have said. I don't say one thing and contradict myself by saying something else a few minutes later. Also my thinking is congruent with my thought patterns. There is harmony to how I feel in response to stimuli, and my actions tend to fit within standards that I maintain for myself. The researchers could finally get a handle on the Korean problem when they realized that the tests showed there is little correlation across the four categories. So my actions, if I'm a normal person, aren't very consistent with my feelings . What I think doesn't necessarily bear much weight on what I say. Congruency across those categories just isn't the name of the game. Thus a soldier can feel loyalty at the emotional level and yet physically respond to brainwashing and do disloyal acts.

So to prepare soldiers for resisting brainwashing, psychologists found they had to concentrate on the area the army was concerned with—actions. They had to train the soldiers to deal with brainwashing actively. It wasn't enough to prepare the soldiers emotionally to resist. Since it was behavior they were interested in, they concentrated on teaching them to act the right way. With little expected correlation between the emotions and actions, they had to train these soldiers like Pavlov's dog, using behavior modification techniques: as soon as something triggered brainwashing categories they had to be ready to respond automatically with loyal behavior.

Thus our soldiers went to Vietnam much better prepared to cope, behavior-wise, with Oriental brainwashing. Outwardly. In a way they were just brainwashed in reverse. They were not supposed to make their own responses for which they could have felt pride or guilt. They responded like Pavlov's dogs. But what happened is that Vietnam became for many an emotional disaster, because their emotions were not prepared to be loyal and they found the bifurcation between their actions and their emotional response to be schizophrenic.

Listening to Paula, I was struck with how demeaning it was for the military to do this to people who were already risking their lives. But like Jim Jones, these military leaders must have seen this precious gift of free will as an overwhelming threat to their own authority. I remember the awful accusation made by Leo Ryan's administrative assistant that at Jonestown they discovered highly sophisticated mind-control drugs which some felt were being provided to Jim Jones by the American military who were interested in experimenting with these, but were afraid to try to do this on American soil. This was hushed up and nothing much came of the accusation—or any real investigation of Jonestown—but it gave me pause. What awful depths to go to in order to win. What a hollow victory we are willing to settle for.

No matter whether you are a parent, a teacher or a military commander, it is natural not to want to cope with the serendipity of that moment when the offspring sits on the edge of the nest—in danger of plummeting off to the depths—or ready to soar off to heights never reached by the parents or those in control. The fledgling may go to places those in power can never follow. Find hidden valleys beyond the mountains and see sights they'll never be able to describe adequately to those back home.

And so in pride there are parents and church leaders and college professors and army psychologists who say: Don't do it your way, do it my way. My way is the only right way, that's why you have to become a robot I can control and that I fcan feel safe and good about. My kingdom will be extended, my power furthered, my audience widened, my side victorious. And should my kingdom be threatened then it is better for you to die.

That's really what authoritarian types are saying—whether in the church, in the army, in the family or in society. Not everyone drinks the cyanide Kool-aid, but there are a lot of ways to destroy someone other than by killing them physically. It kills the church slowly when you don't allow the members to become aware of their own power, exercising their free will. If the congregational members never have to make ethical decisions but only obey rules that are made for them, they will never become productive members of the church. Nor will they become elders who can be models for the younger generation, or even parents capable of raising children who can make ethical choices. The church, the society or the family stagnates when all the power and authority rests with one or two people.

On the mission field those missionaries who try to maintain complete control over their work have what is euphemistically called limited success. If they could trust the Holy Spirit more to work and direct the lives of the different offspring with the church, they would start chains of raising Christian children who grow to understand their free will, and then in turn these would go on to raise other Christian children in the same pattern. This is how the early church obviously grew in the terrific way it did—without TV, printed books, lesson plans or international conferences to beef it all up!

Learning to trust God with the fledglings would also keep Western missionaries from being accused of triumphalism—coming as victorious possessors of the truth, imposing law and order on the vanquished. So often missionaries and church leaders are seen to have some deep-seated desire to be unquestioned and unchallenged.

Maybe the sin of Jim Jones is a societal sin—where those in authority have never wanted to develop the free will of those at the base. They are threatened by anyone who begins to flex this most precious gift given us by our Creator. Anyone who tries to keep another Christian from learning how to exercise their free will, does not trust the Holy Spirit's power to teach and bring that person to maturity.

Being responsible for one's own behavior is risky. The possibility as we sit on the edge of the nest staring at the steep drop is scary. God knows that and promises to undergird us with his supporting wings. Even though the security of such an operation rests on our ability to trust God's promises, the rewards are soaring.

My toes toasted warm that evening by the fireplace at Sequoia, but my heart remained frigidly constricted by the hurt of Jonestown and the hurt of our churches which cripple the offspring, offering them security in exchange for their freedom, cutting their wings so they can't fly higher to where it's at.

Chapter _____ 5

The Andean Marauders

Flying into Lima, Peru, is like flying backwards in a time machine. When I first landed in Peru in 1962 on my way to Brazil as a novice missionary, I only spent a day there, but it was enough to conjure up the memories I had of the Colombia of my childhood—boys hanging onto the rears of ancient streetcars in order to get a precarious free ride, potholed roads that barely allowed for passage, ancient and dank Spanish buildings brooding behind barricaded windows and walls. There were myriad street vendors—always a sign of a depressed economy—and, of course, ill-clad beggars on every hand.

Lima is a dry, virtually rainless city nurtured on water brought down from the faraway Andean peaks, so the only vegetation one finds tends to be in irrigated fields and watered lawns. There is a large hill on the outskirts of town which convinces you that Peruvians are telling the truth when they say it *never* rains—for it is a mountain of dried mud with nary a weed on its caked slopes. The desert of Southern California which gaily blooms each spring from winter rains—songsters to the contrary—looks like the Garden of Eden in comparison.

Returning to Peru almost 20 years after my first visit, I was on assignment doing some investigative reporting for the Marianist Brothers and Priests from Baltimore. Their missionaries in Peru had been sending reports north of how the Carnation and Nestle companies had been manipulating the milk industry of Peru and had aggravated the weakened economy so that now it was practically impossible for any but the wealthy to buy fresh milk for their children to drink. As part of their mission vision various Catholic orders were trying to bring some ethical standards to those American companies whose policies were impacting Catholic congregations in the Third World. Since the Order owned shares in Carnation, the Marianists wanted to get their facts straight before bringing a shareholders resolution to the company's next annual meeting asking for redress.

I was happy to take on the assignment because increasingly I had been bothered by the question of just what my responsibility was—as an American citizen—for the nefarious deeds of American transnational corporations around the world. This first came up when I was still in Brazil and had become acquainted with some Catholic nuns, priests and layworkers who considered it their religious duty to stop what they thought were immoral practices on the part of large Western corporations who were building for themselves high-technology global empires, but in the process becoming so powerful that no small Third World nation could withstand their machinations.

In spearheading this Carnation investigation, I found myself trying to unravel a complicated problem and was directed to some Peruvian economists, professors at the Catholic University in Lima. They were conducting academic research projects investigating—from the vantage point of Peruvian scholars—the effects transnational corporations were having on the Peruvian economy. Often they disagreed with the appraisals of North Atlantic economists, who they felt did not understand the cultural implications.

These Peruvian economists were most cordial to me and shared their insights during long conversations, but they insisted that I also had to meet the people who were being affected by Carnation's company policies. Only then could I understand the passion of the theologians who saw these members of their churches victimized by Carnation et al. I will never forget the stories of the Peruvian people I met through these church contacts.

When the sun comes up each morning behind the humble home of Gregorio and Isabel Cruzado who live in one of the crowded shantytowns girdling Lima, you can slowly begin seeing this family's misery emerge from the unelectrified darkness. As the light improves, the worry lines on Gregorio's face come into focus as he hunches over the twig-burning stove. Except for a crudely made table and a bench lining one wall, the Cruzados have no furniture. Pallets on the floor in the corner serve as beds. The family's entire wardrobe could be stored in a shopping bag.

Gregorio drinks a cup of local herb tea and quickly leaves the dirt-floored shack, not quite knowing where to go to try his luck this day. A bricklayer by trade, he hasn't been able to find steady work for over three years. Yesterday he didn't work, and if something doesn't turn up today, once again the children will cry from hunger. And once again he and Isabel will be powerless to solve their personal dilemma.

Each day thousands of unemployed Peruvians mill in the streets scrounging for their daily bread. Gregorio joins their lot because he has no desire to stay home. He knows too well how the scene will be played: Isabel is thinner than he can ever remember, with sunken eyes which poignantly tell her story. Yet at breakfast she won't eat any bread—in order to leave a bit more for their three surviving children (two others died as infants). At lunch nothing but a few vegetables will embellish their watery soup. A boiled sweet potato divided between the children will give them something hot to chew on. At night the soup will be reheated, and with luck, some tea and bread will finish the family's daily ration. No milk. No eggs. Scarcely any protein.

Gregorio and Isabel's situation is not unique. Story after story could be told about the small people in Peru, people who suffer, right now. Mostly they suffer because Peru is a country that is starving to death. Slowly. That means people don't necessarily die of hunger but of starvation-related diseases. Tuberculosis, for example, has reached pandemic proportions. In some areas, officials say, one out of four is infected with TB. And although Peru once had free clinics and medicines for the poor, it no longer can afford to give such health care to those who need it.

Maria Alvez, mother of three, from the nearby village of Joven de Callao was diagnosed as being tubercular three years ago, but she had little money for proper medication and there was no hospital which would admit her. Finally, when she had advanced tuberculosis, she was admitted to the San Juan de Dios Hospital. But the family could no longer pay her bill, so the hospital forced her to leave.

A hospital official told Miguel, her husband, that if he would pay 5,000 soles (about $20) toward her bill, they would readmit her. To Miguel that amounted to a fortune, but he knew the suffering Maria was going through. In desperation he sold one of their three blankets and some used clothes and then managed to borrow the rest. When Miguel brought Maria and the 5,000 soles to the hospital, they reneged and said there was no bed available then for Maria.

After an interminable effort, Maria was at last admitted to the Loayza Hospital. But by then her pain was beyond relief. She died the month before I met her husband, leaving him with another programmed death: their youngest child, a two-year-old boy, also tubercular. Besides the three children Miguel had to feed and care for, he also had an additional debt of 13,500 soles (about $54) for Maria's coffin. His job as a fish cleaner and sometime stevedore gave him little hope of soon paying off the bill.

At the wake, Miguel said to the priest, "Padre, in your prayer, don't tell the people it was God's will for my wife to die. She wouldn't be dead if we had had food to eat!"

In 1981 out of a population of 20 million, an estimated 20,000 people died from tuberculosis—an increase of more than 4,000 since 1972. Peru has more tubercular deaths than any country in the world. But as Maria's husband knew so well, the majority of these deaths could have been avoided by proper nutrition and health care.

The World Health Organization (WHO) says that to lead a normal life, adults need 2500 to 2800 calories a day, including 56 to 70 grams of protein. In 1974, Peruvians consumed an average of 2251 calories. But by 1980, the average caloric intake was down to 1560. In 1974, Peruvians averaged 56 grams of protein. A decade later this has been reduced to only 26 grams of protein a day—less than half the WHO's standards for a normal life.

These appalling statistics go on and on. But they explain why so much of Lima shares the unmitigated stench of poverty. Garbage is poured onto the middle dividers of the roads so that it will be easier for the people to root through and find something in that fetid heap which they can eat. Almost half the children are malnourished. A third of all pregnant women have anemia. Almost half the deaths that occur in Peru are of children under five. (In Sweden, only two percent of all deaths are of young children.)

I was invited to attend a grass roots Christian community meeting in one of the slum parishes of Lima. After the Bible reading the subject turned to death. An old lady said, "Me! I've lived enough. I'm ready to die. Old people are closer to death."

A young girl across the room answered immediately, "No, little grandmother. That was before. Now it is the children who are closer to death."

Everyone sat silently acknowledging the seriousness of the situation. But what to do?

The sidewalks are filled with people barking wares of every variety, trying to interest someone in buying something that will put a little food on the table. But extreme poverty, which Peruvians might want to hide from their neighbors and friends, becomes apparent in the open-air market.

Carmen Perez, short of stature with high cheekbones which bespeak her Incan ancestors, arrives at the market carrying a baby on her back. A three-year-old walks by her side. She slips the baby out of her shawl and stretches it out on the ground with a few lemons and some chilis and sits back to wait for a sale.

The baby crawls around in the dirt, getting grubbier as the day wears on. In the booths around her, meat remains unsold, but the bones go quickly. Housewives ask the price of chickens but buy only the innards to put some flavor in the pot.

Scarcely anyone can afford even the pork trimmings anymore. Celery leaves, carrot tops, and radish greens are all sold separately. Fish heads, fins, and tails have individual prices, because one can't always afford the rest.

In the bustle of the marketplace, Carmen hears someone haggling about the price of a half tomato. Everything tells the same story: Peru is a country of pathetically hungry people.

I walked through the dusty hovels that make up so much of Lima wondering what had brought this once-proud country, which spawned the majestic Inca Empire, to virtual bankruptcy. Why are so few resources left for even simple survival? Why must people like Isabel and Gregorio struggle so hard for so little food? And what has this to do with Carnation and Nestle? And with me and all the good Christian people I know in America?

My first conclusion, in the face of this suffering, was that we must indeed live in a world gone mad. But the more I talked to Peruvians, the more I saw that it isn't so much a world gone mad as a world gone greedy.

As you look at the facts, the reasons for Peru's fate become painfully clear. And one of the major causes for the suffering of people like Maria and Carmen and Isabel and Gregorio— and the others— is the structure of the world economic system which allows for the systematic exploitation of the Third World by major transnational corporations.

Under the guise of developing the underdeveloped, international bankers hope to appear alturistic. There is growing evidence to show such "altruism" needs to be questioned: developing the Third World might make luxury items and a modernized Western life-style available for the upper classes in the country, but in the process the peasant farmers lose their land, the blue-collar workers face ever-increasing levels of unemployment and middle-class entrepreneurs are often forced out of business. And if any dare question the system, they are labeled Communists.

Tracing Carnation's history in Peru was a depressing task for I learned firsthand how such exploitation works. Carnation came to Peru 50 years ago. During this half century, the California-based company of the contented cow has manipulated Peru's milk industry for its own benefit, significantly reduced the amount of milk available to the poor of Peru, and sucked excessive profits out of the country.

Carnation controls the milk industry of southern Peru, while the smaller milk production of northern Peru is controlled by Nestle. How Carnation achieved that control— and what it has done with it— has been the subject of much research. Gonzalo Arroyo, a professor from the University of Paris at Nanterre, and Manuel Lajo, a professor from the Pontifical Catholic University of Lima, have looked closely at Carnation's role in the milk industry and written widely acclaimed academic papers on this subject. These economists contend that when Carnation came into the country it systematically ran its competition out of business by paying producers more than the going rate of the area. Consequently almost none of the independent, locally-owned dairies and creameries are still in business.

Another ploy Carnation used on arrival in Peru to induce the local producers into selling their milk exclusively to Carnation was to promise to supply their milk producers with that famed American technical assistance and sophisticated know-how in order to upgrade their stock and garner more profits. These producers now claim that virtually none of these promises materialized.

Any potential dairy competitors who have tried to establish milk-processing factories in the area have been repeatedly thwarted in their attempts with underhanded tactics. The local press accuses both Carnation and Nestle of being in cahoots with international bankers and the military—who until recently have had a dictatorship in the country and still wield immense control—in seeing that no one else ever gets the necessary funding or governmental approval to build a competing factory facility for milk processing.

These are all considered normal industry procedures by successful businessmen. And once Carnation had its monopoly firmly in hand, the next step was a foregone conclusion: it began reducing the price it paid its milk producers. There was no reason for the dairy owners to strike or protest such a reduction because by then they had nowhere else to sell their product and no other avenue to the consumer. Carnation and Nestle were in a place where they could dictate the entire scenario.

And in fact Carnation then tightened its manipulative hold even further, playing even dirtier pool: It began refusing to buy large quantities of milk the local producers had for sale. This served as a softening technique, and in the face of bankruptcy and inability to pay their bills, the milk producers were forced to accept even lower prices. Finally these unethical moves drove many of the independent producers out of business. It surprised few people that many Carnation executives began buying these dairy farms at depressed prices.

When Carnation refused to buy huge quantities of milk from the producers in southern Peru, it also refused to sell milk in Lima and the other urban centers. This shortage helped Carnation in another softening move—preparing the public for a substantial rise in the price of milk to the consumer. At one period, over 12,000 liters of milk were being poured *daily* into rivers in rural Peru because of Carnation's policy, while fresh milk was unobtainable in the capital city. This did not go unnoticed by the Peruvian press or by the parents of many needy and malnourished children. It also fanned anti-gringo feelings among those who saw themselves victimized by greedy Western business tactics.

The press also was irate because although milk prices are technically set by the government, the committee that decides those prices includes representatives from Carnation and Nestle but does not include a representative to speak for the consumer. As a result, the committee accepts the industry's figures and their reports of costs as well as the industry's requests for milk prices without investigating what their true costs or profits might be.

With milk prices having gone up some 500% over the five years preceding my visit to Peru, I found that the majority of young children in Lima had never had a chance to drink fresh milk. Not surprisingly, milk consumption in Peru had dropped to a quarter of what it had been five years before, reaching a level that was less than a quarter of the absolute minimum Peru's National Institute of Nutrition recommends for children.

Such vicious practices of course rankled Christian missionaries in the area, and they refused to call these capitalistic business practices "good". No wonder many church people began to question how Christians could export a system which is based on the principle that the consumer must beware! That might be OK in the Western world where education and experience make the consumer and the vendor matched adversaries. But if the consumers are illiterate, trusting and powerless victims in a Third World country, they have no tools at their disposal that allow them *to* beware. So increasingly religious groups such as the Marianists have decided that their Christian duty obliges them to become a voice for the voiceless, and thus they put energy into trying to call corporations like Carnation to task.

Another concern the religious community had regarding the milk industry in Peru was that this is one of the few countries in the world where the majority of the processed milk sold comes as canned evaporated milk. This is an expensive, less nutritious form of milk, but it is a very profitable, convenient system for Carnation. It not only lets Carnation use outdated, antiquated, inefficient equipment salvaged from their operations in other countries where they have been forced by consumer demands to modernize, but it requires no refrigeration or prompt selling of the product. With the government automatically setting the price of milk at a cost-plus-profit level, and with its monopoly of the market, Carnation has not had any incentive to improve their setup.

Also since Carnation has no competition in southern Peru, it has been able to condition the urban population to take milk in the form that it offers, even if it is less beneficial to their health and a lot more expensive, making it even harder for the poor to purchase milk for their children. Again the unforgivable sin in this story is that the real victims remain the children of Peru.

To make the story even seamier, instead of buying what milk it used for this canning process from Peruvian producers, and in order not to have to be dependent on the milk producers in the south, Carnation began importing much of its milk from its own subsidiaries in New Zealand in the form of dry milk solids. This was then reconstituted and evaporated, and finally this highly processed concoction was put into cans to sell to the few consumers who could afford it. Currently Carnation's canned milk in Peru is 60% evaporated reconstituted dry milk solids. And because of sweet-talking legal machinations, Carnation was even able to buy this foreign dry milk at a government-subsidized price, thus further hurting the local farmers and increasing its own winnings all around.

So while Peruvian milk producers were forced to dump milk because no one would process it, Carnation was importing subsidized dry milk solids from a First World country, adding to Peru's unfavorable trade balance and contributing further to the economic privation of the people.

The virulent editorials in Peru's press thus became understandable to me as I traced Carnation's crimes against this country. Professor Lajo patiently tried to explain to an economics novice like me how the negative trade balance to which Carnation contributes again mainly hurts those at the low end of the economic spectrum. This negative trade balance leaves the government with virtually no funds to pay for social services of any kind— medicines for the tubercular, adequate wages for schoolteachers, passable roads for the local people. Instead of using their tax revenues for such services which would benefit the general public, the government earmarks this revenue mainly for foreign banks to pay interest on loans for unnecessary, sophisticated defense items, and luxury goods imported for the benefit of a small percentage of the population.

And instead of allowing Peruvian milk companies to handle the industry, the government places it in the hands of Western transnational corporations which neither reinvest their earnings in the country nor help the nation develop at any level. Companies like Carnation and Nestle take out of Peru what little hard currency is generated as their lawful profit— and piously claim to be benefiting and developing Peru in the process. But while the rest of the country faces national bankruptcy, Carnation never loses. Government policies guarantee them a profit, which they always send north. In addition to this profit, the Peruvian operation is also permitted to send generous royalties to the American head office for use of their name, their processes and their technology.

At one point when the price of Carnation's Peruvian milk (marketed under the *Leche Gloria* label) went so high that few could afford to buy it, because of its burgeoning warehouses Carnation asked for and received permission from the government to begin exporting its milk to other countries. But fortunately the outcry from a hungry populace was so great the government finally rescinded its approval. This was a good lesson, especially for academicians, who realized that at some point the government was responsive to the voice on the streets. And this also motivated the missionaries in Peru to ask for an investigation, because at some point you must hope that one person or one group can make a difference. Christ certainly taught this.

I have never understood why many church people feel threatened when someone begins to question the ethics of international capitalist practices. The policies that led Carnation to dump milk in Peru show that Carnation's true interest is not in developing the Peruvian people or helping them toward an American style of life. The principles of supply and demand, which are supposed to keep greedy producers like Carnation in check, are not based on biblical precepts but on Adam Smith's. Thus it should be OK to question whether these principles are in need of revision.

Obviously in much of our modern world, Adam Smith's principles no longer cover the bases: The access of transnational producers to government, monopolistic markets and excessive power allows them to transcend the normal pressures of the marketplace that heretofore, according to Smith, would have kept their goods within reasonable reach of most consumers.

These are changing times and it is the moral obligation of all Christians to feed the hungry, clothe the naked and visit the sick— especially when their plight is the direct result of companies such as Carnation. Of course, the blame for Peru's troubles doesn't lie solely with Carnation. Other transnational corporations have used similar methods to extort excessive profits from the poor of Peru. And much of the blame for the country's bankruptcy must be placed on the powerful elite and the military who have been accused of personal corruption and profiteering from their relationships with Western companies.

In my travels around Latin America I have rubbed shoulders with these incredibly wealthy people who have no compunctions about their extravagant life-style. Taking a Concorde to Paris for a dinner engagement and returning the next day, means nothing to them. The shops in Miami are favorite haunts for them and they often fly in for a weekend to spend thousands of dollars on clothes, accessories and electronic items before returning home to the maids and gardeners they underpay and regard as completely expendable.

This same kind of attitude extends up to the government levels. While the military has controlled the Peruvian government for much of the past two decades, when it could find no money to provide health care for the poor, it was able to find money to purchase expensive, unnecessary defense weapons—their electronic toys grown big. Since they buy these from the United States and other arms-producing countries, no one cares that these arms sales keep the Marias of Peru who are dying of tuberculosis from receiving adequate health care.

With its excessive arms spending alongside the extravagant importation of luxury items for a few wealthy people, Peru at one time had the second largest per capita debt in the world. International banks then cracked down, refusing to extend additional credit. As a result, Peru had to tighten the belt economically. But as in most cases of national economy, it was the little people—the uneducated, the young and the poor—who suffered. And as with Gregorio, Isabel, Maria, Miguel, Carmen and the old lady—they don't always know the full reasons for their suffering. But they are woefully aware they are starving.

By the time I came back from Peru, I was as upset as the Marianists were about the situation and agreed to organize a shareholders resolution that would question Carnation specifically about their practices in the Third World. It was a simple request, asking the company to provide information about its policies in certain dubious areas.

One real concern was the infant formula controversy. Carnation at that time in Peru touted its thoroughly unnutritious *Leche Gloria* evaporated milk as an infant food— even though WHO guidelines strictly forbade anyone to claim evaporated milk as an infant food. I brought back from Peru cans of Carnation's *Leche Gloria* that listed the recommended dilution for babies of different ages.

It seemed like dirty pool to me to have their advertising programs— which used a lot of radio ads on popular programs— aimed at uneducated Third World mothers, implying to these mothers that by using such modern and Western products they would produce healthy and strong children, when the exact reverse was true. Since most mothers could not afford to follow the formula instructions— let alone read them— they assumed this American milk was some kind of modern magical potion that would produce smiling, healthy babies like the ones on the posters flooding the corner markets. The Bottle Death syndrome began popping up here in Peru as it has done all over the world.

I should have known that these formal enquiries with Carnation would fall on deaf ears. Most of Carnation's shares were controlled by various members of the Stuart family (founders of Carnation) who don't feel obligated to answer anybody's questions. The request was turned down— in a rather rude manner. Interestingly enough, several employees approached me after the meeting and congratulated our efforts saying, "Keep up the good work. We'd lose our jobs if we say anything, but we're really glad you're bringing it out in the open." The problem comes: if you quit this job with Carnation, can you expect to find a more ethical company anywhere?

Although it was discouraging to be turned down out of hand, we decided to come back again the next year and through the shareholders' resolution process ask Carnation to set up an Ethical Review Committee where such issues could be addressed by concerned shareholders. This, we pointed out, would also benefit the company's image because they could avoid using practices that have produced so much bad press in the Third World. (In the Philippines, Carnation has been accused of trying to economize by sealing their tin cans with lead plugs— which are illegal in the U.S. because it is proven that this poisons the milk and can cause mental retardation in small children.)

But even within this rather limited circle, Carnation refused to have its practices and policies brought under an ethical scrutiny. There were no questions it was willing to answer: Why does it treat the health of its consumers so casually? Why does it use antiquated, expensive processes in countries that can ill afford them? What incentives are needed to produce cheaper milk for Third World customers?

When Carnation told us they did not feel such questions were worth discussing, I somehow lost a great deal of confidence in the system. What made these large transnational corporations feel they were beyond the pale of criticism and responsibility to the small consumer and the small critic? It was no wonder to me that people in the Third World decry American exploitation, resenting the presence of powerful gringos and their transnational corporations.

This trip to Peru was really an eye-opener for me. I lost a lot of my naivete.

One of the more shocking items was told me by an American Lutheran pastor who had worked in Peru for over a decade. Abroad people in the American community tend to meet one another, so you often find yourself intimate with people who in America would not be in your circle. Consequently this pastor played racquets weekly with an American embassy official and in the process became good friends. One day this embassy friend brought this Lutheran pastor a classified document— asking him please not to reveal the source of this secret information! Instead of war secrets, the paper held a list of the pharamceutical products produced by American firms and sold in Peru but which had *not* been approved by the Federal Drug Administration. These drugs were proscribed for purchase or use by people who worked for the American embassy. This racquets-playing embassy official had asked his superiors if this list could be distributed to the American community, but the ambassador said no.

The only reason he could perceive that the ambassador would make such a decision is that the American government, being medically responsible for its workers, was only interested in not becoming liable for medical expenses or medical suits against themselves. The rest of the American community, to say nothing of the Peruvian public, was not their charge, and the ambassador did not want to interfere with good American business tactics.

As a friendly act, this embassy worker decided to slip the list to his American friend anyway. In a way this could be considered a treasonous act, but this embassy official simply could not in good conscience let a fellow American suffer what the government was more than willing to allow the unsuspecting citizens of Peru suffer.

I was appalled by this tale, and then doubly appalled because on returning to the U.S. from Peru I found that the magazine *Mother Jones* had that same month published an article called "The Corporate Crime of the Century" for which they were awarded the National Magazine Award that year. This piece documented how transnational corporations were systematically dumping in Third World countries banned or hazardous products which the law prohibited their selling in America but which could still turn them a profit if they had a marketplace.

Since then the story has only worsened for in the next couple of years Third World countries, including Bangladesh, have decided that to protect their people from such inhumane practices they would prohibit the importation of these dumped products. Bangladesh in 1982 banned 1,700 drugs it deemed ineffective, unnecessary or hazardous. In response to this, the Pharmaceutical Manufacturers Association of America not only tried to pressure the American government into protecting their interests and coercing the Bangladesh government to rescind, they also threatened to boycott Bangladesh and not send them *any* pharmaceutical products from the West if they weren't allowed to send in the banned products.

With this kind of business ethics coming from the capitalist world it is no wonder that many in the Third World look with awe and respect on Castro's Cuba, which, despite economic difficulties, has been able to provide socialized medicine for everyone, equal opportunity in education, and food for all. The Peruvians I talked to pointed out that life expectancy in Cuba is 71.2 years, just a fraction behind that in the U.S. Peru has an appalling 57 years life expectancy. When you watch your children cry themselves to sleep because they are hungry, trading some of your freedoms for increased food and security seems pretty attractive.

We Americans must become more aware of what our money and our companies are doing in Third World countries like Peru and Bangladesh. As I told a Carnation vice-president during a meeting we had in which we were trying to explain our concerns, "We come from a Judeo-Christian heritage that clearly teaches that we reap what we sow. And we Americans do not like to have to reap what companies like yours are sowing in Peru and the Third World." (How many Americans enjoyed the agonizing 400 days when our hostages were reaping for our nation what Kermit Roosevelt sowed when he went to Iran in 1951 loaded with CIA money and proceeded to illegally establish the Shah in power?)

Fifteen and a half million children die each year. Fifteen million of those are in the Third World. As Christians in a developed nation, we have a responsibility to our neighbors. We cannot pass them by as they lie wounded, tubercular, exploited, hungry and robbed. Binding up their wounds means we must stop these modern-day marauders from stealing their gold, destroying their land, starving their children.

Someday the Lord will say to some, "Depart from me, for I was hungry and you did not feed me" (Mt 25:42). I want to be free of that burden.

Chapter _____ 6

Peace, Justice and Kampuchean Refugees

I was a voracious reader as a child—and loved being taken to Far Eastern climes, while tucked away in my tree house or curled up on pillows in the window seat, by the likes of a Rudyard Kipling, a Joseph Conrad or a Pearl Buck tale. Even though I had lived half my life in South America and had wandered over Europe and the British Isles on several trips, I never felt I could consider myself a world traveler until I had been East and seen at least a few of those mythical places. Therefore I was excited when an assignment came my way which took me to Thailand.

Bangkok was just what I had fantasized—hot and humid, pedicabs scurrying through incredibly congested traffic, filigreed Buddhist temples with spires rising to the clouds. The Thai were short, slight and very gracious. Even though I could not read the street signs or understand their alphabet, I felt surrounded by people who cared that I see and experience a city they obviously loved and were proud of.

I was scheduled to join some volunteer relief workers who were going to inaugurate an experimental program in the Cambodian— or as they now wanted to be called, Kampuchean— refugee camps on the eastern borders of Thailand. It was a rather creative relief project aimed at alleviating some of the terrible food shortages in Kampuchea by sending into the country simple farm implements and seed over what they were calling the land bridge.

During the years when Pol Pot had control of the Kampuchean government (1975-1979) the borders had been completely closed with no traffic or communication allowed out of the country. However, word leaked out inevitably of the terrible carnage which was taking place under his crazed Communist dictatorship. The rumors were gruesomely confirmed when the Vietnamese Communist government, provoked by border incidents with their rabid neighbors, finally decided to invade and stabilize the situation in Kampuchea.

The lines of communication between Kampuchea and the rest of the world were opened by the Vietnamese who also began allowing some aid into the country. But since they were leery of Western relief workers, the Vietnamese had been slow in issuing visas, and only a handful of Westerners were working in the country. In turn, most relief agencies were hesitant to send in unsupervised aid.

A working compromise finally evolved when the Vietnamese, who did not officially approve, turned their backs as thousands of refugees— most on the verge of starvation— began to cross the Thai border. A dozen impromptu refugee camps sprang up all along that border so relief agencies— the United Nations High Commission for Refugees (UNHCR) and other private agencies— could attend to this emergency.

All the years I had lived in the jungles of Brazil, we had very little access to modern communication devices, yet early on I became impressed with the efficiency of the jungle telegraph. Somehow important news manages to travel quickly down those jungle trails. This was certainly true in Kampuchea. Once the first refugees found succor on the Thai border, there had been a steady stream of Khmers arriving in the camps, until now they held an estimated 350,000 refugees. The Thai army cordoned off a limited area around the border to contain the refugees and everyone leaving or entering this zone had to have special permission.

The weak and infirm Khmers who managed to make it to these refugee camps often were brought in large wooden wheeled carts which appeared to come straight out of the Middle Ages. Though springless and terribly uncomfortable, these quaint, anachronistic oxen-pulled carts were really the only way for anyone from this bankrupt land—with no access to gasoline—to travel over those muddy, rutted tracks through the Kampuchean jungles. After these carts brought their passengers with their meager belongings to the camps, they often turned around to go back to bring other relatives or friends out to the camps, taking any foodstuffs they could beg, barter or scrounge.

Some of the relief agencies decided that such ox carts could become ideal vehicles for a land-bridge project, for they could be loaded on this return trip to Kampuchea with elementary farm implements, seed and fishing gear—what farmers needed to survive in that land. Incredibly, even primitive tools had virtually disappeared under the mayhem of the Pol Pot regime which considered such items bourgeois, so that just owning them became a criminal act.

This land bridge program would also help stem the stream of refugees, because when their fertile land—once known as the rice bowl of Indochina—was in production, these people could again feed themselves. All this was explained to me by John Dennis, an American relief worker, as we drove out to the border for what I was assured would be a fascinating weekend.

On Saturday we stopped in to meet Tiradaet Muengaew. Monday morning the newspapers reported he was dead. That news turned a fact-finding lark into a serious pause which left me asking repeatedly, "When will justice and peace reign on this earth?"

Tiradaet climbed out of the army bunker to greet us after the guard at the gate asked on his walkie-talkie for permission to let us pass. He was clad in baggy army regulation cotton pants and a white T-shirt with his name stenciled on it. We were shown to a breezeway between two storage sheds and sat on straight-backed chairs around a rectangular coffee table: Tiradaet, John Dennis, Greg Bunker—a newly-arrived veterinarian from New Zealand—and I. A couple of Thai soldiers stood behind us curiously listening as John explained to Tiradaet the new agricultural project for Nong Chan—the nearby refugee camp sheltering 50,000 Kampucheans which John and the others had chosen as the first gate for the land bridge into Kampuchea.

It was a courtesy call. We had already received official permission from the Army Chief of Staff in Bangkok, but Tiradaet was the local commander and it was important to stay in his good graces. Tiradaet looked to me like a young kid. Later the papers named him a captain, so his appearance must have belied his age.

Not understanding a word of Thai, I felt strangely as though I were deaf—able to perceive the visual imagery but only conjecture on its meaning. Looking around, I realized this was my first time in a real war zone and a real army bunker. An ashtray on the coffee table, the only decoration, was made of bullets standing on end welded together—it added to the impression that these were not toy guns the soldiers casually carried on their shoulders, nor was this a peaceful spot of the earth.

The men in Tiradaet's command were just as curious about who we were as I was about them, but we stared at each other without smiling. I have wondered since whether they had any intimations of their approaching death. It certainly was not a time for cutesy chatter.

Hot and humid, the afternoon air lay heavy and still, adding to the ominous feelings. I took out a Chinese folding fan trying to create my own air conditioning. John handed Tiradaet his business card—printed with the Latin alphabet on one side and the rune-like Thai script on the other. Then as Tiradaet wrote a note down for John—in my deafness I knew not what—I noticed the intricately worked 24-karat gold ring with a large ruby-colored stone Tiradaet was wearing and wondered at its meaning. The gold certainly looked real, the stone probably was too. An expensive ring for that stark setting, I thought—and hardly what you wore with T-shirts.

Later John, our old hand fluent in Thai, explained that a lot of gold was being brought across the border by Kampucheans to trade for rice, foodstuffs and Thai consumer products. Since these refugees were prime candidates for being gouged—even King Midas found out that the abundance of gold doesn't keep you from starving--it was illegal for anyone other than government-appointed agents to deal in precious metals. Two volunteer relief workers—European doctors—had been arrested and shipped back home a few weeks previously for possessing some silver elephants.

In spite of such vigilance, trading in precious commodities was rampant in the border area, and John said a lot of people were sprouting new jewelery! Sadly, the Angkor Wat temple ruins, only 60 miles on the other side of the border, were also being stripped.

The Vietnamese apparently cared little about Kampuchean heritage and culture and were allowing the Khmers to loot the temple artifacts. These showed up in Thailand where they were bartered on the black market for foodstuffs. It depressed me to hear. And I wished I knew the answer to my justice and peace question.

As we filed out of the sentry post, Captain Tiradaet suggested we stop at another bunker down the road and pay our respects to the corporal who was immediately responsible for the refugee camp. He radioed ahead to alert him we were coming. There was an impressive collection of sophisticated equipment being used in these remote parts!

Walking back to the van, I saw some touch-sensitive mimosa which I remembered from my childhood in Colombia. I stooped to show John and Greg this fern-like plant whose leaves fold up immediately on touch. Years after leaving Colombia I learned in biology that an electric stimulus from the slightest touch triggered the plant's turgor pressure mechanism. But even understanding the system did not detract from its fascination. And somehow finding a link to my own history made this army post appear slightly less hostile.

Our van had been left parked under the blazing tropical sun, and I knew it would be like an oven. Pent, our Thai driver, stood alongside waiting patiently. In the tropics sitting inside a vehicle parked in the sun is tantamount to braising yourself— whereas standing outside, the slightest breeze can help cool you. Roongroj, a Thai working for the Oxfam Relief people as their purchasing agent, waited with him. Neither wanted up-close contact with the army types. Both Peng and Roongroj were pleasant and conscientious workers, but their eyes were serious and sad— and I wondered what they had seen to give them those eyes. I soon found out.

All day I had been struck by the similarities to the jungle interior of Brazil: the rusty strips of jungle road holding back the encroaching lush vegetation on either side, the sticky heat, the red leached sandy soil, and the bits of virgin forest still standing showing the familiar tall hardwood trees. It was also a familiar relief when cumulus clouds periodically covered the face of the sun, cooling the land.

There were differences: water buffalo wallowing in flooded rice fields and a water-filled moat which stretched north and south for 40 kilometers along the border which we bridged to enter the refugee camp. John said the moat was a tank trap—the dirt from the ten-foot deep ditch piled high on the Thai side so that any tank wanting to invade Thailand from the Cambodian border would either have to cross it on these patrolled roads or have to bridge not just the moat, but then climb the steep embankment on the other side and be vulnerably exposed on the horizon. The Thai certainly did not trust Pol Pot, and the Vietnamese were traditional enemies.

Once on the other side of the moat we were in the Nong Chan refugee camp which was built on old rice paddies. Now with the summer monsoon, the camp appeared to be a giant checkerboard adrift. The square paddies, separated by raised ridges which had once helped the farmers irrigate their fields, were all flooded. On this soggy plot of land two and a half kilometers wide and three kilometers long lived 50,000 people.

Instead of a tent city, it was a thatch city—row after row of thatch-roofed bamboo sleeping platforms raised barely above the flooded ground. Someone had provided acres of blue plastic which many used to cover the roofs to keep the monsoon rains at bay. A few huts had walls of woven mats giving them a more permanent appearance, but most had nothing to protect the inhabitants from the driving rains. Families of four were allotted platforms two by three meters long. Standing up inside their homes was a luxury few afforded.

John and Greg were very pleased. We had sailed through all the checkpoints with a car, a van and a loaded truck without being stopped, searched or harassed. Tiradaet had even confirmed our permission to stay in a house rented by the Oxfam people in Koke Sung, only two kilometers away from Nong Chan. All other volunteer workers lived in Aranyaprathet, some 25 kilometers distant, arriving at eight each morning, leaving by six. There were distinct advantages to Aranyaprathet—electricity and running water, restaurants and grocery stores, telephones and paved roads—and 25 kilometers of buffer from the border clashes that sporadically flared when night fell giving cover to wandering Pol Pot guerrillas, the Vietnamese-supported Heng Samrin government forces or the Thai border patrols. Since an unwritten agreement seemed to limit this firefighting to the hours of curfew—8 PM to 6 AM—the relief agencies as well as the civilians living in the area did not feel overly threatened as long as they stayed indoors.

Oxfam had decided to establish a base at Koke Sung in order to set up a crude and temporary cart-repair shop within easy access to the camp. The village's lack of amenities reminded me of the eleven years I had lived in the jungles without electricity. But I knew adjusting to such a life-style was easy—look at the millions of people around the world who live contentedly just that way!

We had left the truck and van unloading in Koke Sung to head for the camp to make sure that the operations were go for the cattle vaccination scheduled for the next day. Walking down the main thoroughfare of Nong Chan, I was overwhelmed by a prevailing, acrid stench throughout the camp produced by too many bodies, too many animals in too small, too hot and too wet a spot with no drainage available for sewage. Incredible swarms of flies consequently were everywhere. I was told they had been worse. A recent outbreak of cholera had resulted in a lot of insecticides being sprayed, but I still had never seen so many flies—swarming, lighting, bothering.

John was looking for Virat, a Thai-speaking Khmer refugee in Nong Chan who acted as his interpreter. As we walked along, John pointed out a barbershop—just another thatch roof held up by slim poles, a mirror hanging on a woven mat wall, a chair, a towel and some scissors. What more did you need? The bicycle repair shop was easier to identify: several young men were standing around upended bicycles while the mechanic looked like mechanics do around the world—slightly grubby and greasy, yet confidently knowledgeable.

The jungle telegraph was as efficient as ever and Virat suddenly appeared and was introduced. While John discussed their game plan for the next day, I wandered into the hospital we had just passed. A Red Cross flag flew from a tall bamboo pole in front of the largest thatch-and-pole structure in the camp. Dirt fill had obviously been brought in to raise the level of the ground because the hard-packed floor was dry. Beds made of plywood pallets on bamboo frames were set in long rows with just enough room to walk in between. The woven mat walls let plenty of fresh air and light through—probably a pretty efficient system for the tropics.

An Irish nun/nurse, Sister Joy Riordan, kindly led me around the "hospital", making this harrowing scene somehow human. I tried hard to emulate her matter-of-fact acceptance of it all. The young man writhing in pain was waiting for transportation to take him to a real hospital in Aranyaprathet for an operation—he had a urethral obstruction. She stopped to give a wailing baby something for pain and to make sure the mother knew that they had to go to the hospital, too. I tried not to grimace when the nurse gently examined the screaming baby's swollen testicles. The mother cooed and rocked him trying to transfer the pain, like mothers do around the world.

At a corner bed Sister Joy stopped, "Here's our oldest refugee!"

Granny Morn was 87. She had arrived the week before suffering from beriberi and severe malnutrition. The nun was especially pleased with Granny's progress. She had been brought from the nearby province of Battambang, three days by oxcart. "She's a tough old lady to survive all that she's been through."

Granny sat up to greet me, her black eyes sparkling with life. Granny's son had been in France studying when Pol Pot came to power. Returning home, he was killed along with her two sons-in-law. Her husband died, but Granny said you couldn't blame Pol Pot for that— he was old. Six grandchildren had died of malnutrition leaving her with two daughters and a grandson. I asked Sister Joy why Granny's teeth were stained dark. She didn't know, but speculated it was some jungle bark Granny chewed constantly.

Sister Joy introduced me to a French pediatrician, Henriette Chamouillet from Lyon, who told me that one of their most irritating frustrations were the parents with sick and dying children who would eat the rations intended for the patients. This forced the nurses to have to add the feeding of the children to their harried schedules if they were to make sure they were properly getting their due.

I couldn't help wondering what I would do if I were starving to death. But it was a dismaying tale. Could it be that with life so precarious, normal parenting no longer was instinctive? Or was civilization broken down when people live at such a marginal level? Somehow I had thought protecting the young was a basic instinct of our race.

I was ready to get out of that hospital and was glad when the nun suggested that I should visit the feeding center across the street where children with malnutrition and lactating mothers were given the second meal of the day. Everyone else in camp got one meal!

On the way out I passed two Red Cross nurses coming in who looked surprisingly like Martians! One had pants rolled up to the knees, the other had on a dress, but both wore tall, mud-caked boots and carried radios with flexible antennae which stood waving a foot above their heads, a camera slung on one shoulder, funny hats clamped tightly over their hair and dark glasses. They had been out making house calls, checking out the camp.

When Greg and John had settled the plans for Sunday, we were ready to hike to the back part of the camp, deep into Kampuchean territory. Down the dusty road we went, passing children playing in the drainage ditches, boys pushing and pulling homemade toys—wheels made of anything round with sticks and strings attached. Somehow a boy's desire for a toy truck or its facsimile is universal to any who have had the slightest contact with the Western world. I was sorry to see a child playing with a cheap plastic submachine gun—surely inappropriate in this setting.

One of the more appalling stories John told us was that the worst Pol Pot killers had been boys ten to 15 years of age. The Chinese, who had offered to train the Pol Pot forces, were furious when "mere children" deplaned in China. Pol Pot insisted that these were his best killers. Certainly as a mother I agreed that we parent into this world barbarians who must learn through education, culture and religion what mercy and humankindness and grace are all about, but it was so criminal to corrupt these youngsters that early to became hardened assassins. No wonder there were so many children in these refugee camps—the parents obviously wanted to whisk them away from such monstrous temptations.

Every time we paused so John could point something out, youngsters would close in on us, tentatively touching, reaching out, grabbing on. As we walked along, they called out, "OK! OK!" as though this American expression somehow linked them to us. Before long the three of us were walking along holding the hands of these cavorting, laughing children who needed to be special, to be noticed and to make contact in that confusing, deranged world.

Leaving the main road, we took off across the narrow ledges between the marshy squares of ex-rice paddies, now oozy mud. Every now and then the ridge was washed out, so I would clutch my camera fiercely and step over a watery chasm. Once I tripped on a root and barely caught myself before falling. It would have been a mess if I had landed in that grubby soup, and I mumbled many thanks to my guardian angels.

Along the way John via Virat would stop and ask someone a question. The back Kampuchean half of Nong Chan was much more a temporary settlement. John and Greg zoomed in on an oxcart being loaded by a young fellow surrounded by a half dozen young women and a passel of children. He had arrived the day before, was loading up today and would start at dawn to go back home. The young women were his relatives— sisters or sisters-in-law who stayed here at the refugee camp to be eligible to collect the rice seed and supplies on distribution days. Whatever they could save from their allotment they sent back to relatives in Kampuchea. I asked them via John via Virat about their families. Virat relayed the information that all these young women were widows!

The news reports I'd read about Kampuchea had made this all seem so far away. Now I was seeing, touching and talking to these people who had suffered through the many ignominies heaped on them by everyone—Americans, Russians, Chinese, Pol Pot, Vietnamese, Khmer Rouge, Khmer Seri, Heng Samrin. What had they done to become the scapegoats of the world?

The area had long been in turmoil. When the Vietnamese had stepped in ostensibly to save the country from itself and from the Pol Pot regime which had massacred or starved nearly a third of the Kampuchean population, most observers attributed the move to the Vietnamese paranoia about their traditional enemy, the Chinese, who were backing the Pol Pot regime and thus controlling yet another stretch of Vietnamese border.

The rationale of the Pol Pot regime was incomprehensible. It was the Chinese Cultural Revolution extrapolated to insane extremes. To eradicate from their land all who "exploited and lived as parasites" they made the capital of Phnom Penh a ghost town, forcing everyone to the countryside to be meaningful contributors of the economic system.

Mercy became an unknown virtue; knowledge a sin. Anyone with any formal education was seen as a suspect enemy of the state, so wearing glasses was a crime worthy of execution because it indicated an educated, thus bourgeois, element. Huge earthen dams were constructed with little technical skill and no equipment because it was a crime to be a technocrat and a sin to have the simplest hoe. The once-sophisticated irrigation system, which had made Kampuchea the largest rice exporter of Southeast Asia before it was destroyed by Americans bombs during the Vietnam war, was left a morass of disorder. Even with forced labor, the fertile, leveed rice land became a wasteland. And the people starved.

When Cambodia was finally opened again by the Vietnamese, relief agencies began airlifting emergency food supplies to Phnom Penh as well as shipping relief goods to the Kampuchean port of Kompong Som. But this was expensive—shipping rice by air cost $1000 per ton. By using the refugees to carry relief supplies overland back home, hopefully a cheaper and quicker distribution channel would be established—a ton of rice ordered in Bangkok cost $250 and was delivered within three days to the Khmer farmers at the Kampuchean border, while a ton shipped from Singapore or China took several weeks to deliver and cost between $400 to $600.

The land bridge also delivered relief goods directly to the rural area which needed the rice seed most. Nong Chan, the major land bridge, is opposite Battambang, Kampuchea's principal rice-producing province. Too, it was safer since Kampuchea was still without a viable transportation system—guerrillas of the left and the right ruled the back roads after dusk and made them precarious by day.

John Dennis was a typical relief worker who had responded to this Kampuchean crisis. He had been a Peace Corps volunteer in Northern Thailand for three and a half years, and now had come back after finishing a master's degree in developmental sociology. Raised on a farm, he had an undergraduate degree in anthropology and had done tropical agricultural experiment work at the University of Florida. During his Peace Corps stint, John wrote a paper which received wide attention because it outlined suitable rice varieties for Southeast Asia.

Greg laughingly told me of John's visit to the U.S. embassy's agricultural division the first week he was back in Thailand to ask for information about new varieties of rice seed now available. He quietly let the embassy person summarize back to him all the cogent facts from his own paper before finally admitting that he was the quoted expert!

His gentle spirit makes John fit well in Thailand where raising your voice is uncouth. His experience in Northern Thailand made him familiar with the needs as well as the mentality of the farmers in the area. Originally headed for Phnom Penh, John like many others was still waiting for his visa, working with the refugees from the Thai side of the border. His knowledge of rice seed qualities—long-stem floating rice for May planting, traditional long-season rice for greater planting latitude and short-stemmed miracle rice for more sophisticated planting techniques—had saved many a relief boondoggle. His contribution was vital, because sending improper seed would be disastrous: the crops would fail and starvation would continue.

Through interviewing peasant Khmer farmers at the various refugee camps, John heard of the absolute dearth of even the most primitive farm implements, and spearheaded the assembling of agricultural packages to send in each cart crossing the border: ten varied-sized hoe heads— he investigated which size and weight the small-statured Khmer farmers preferred— four plowshares, 800 fishhooks, rope and fishnets. Virat was keeping demographic records for them to give a rough idea of where these farm kits where headed.

Throughout Southeast Asia draft animals traditionally have been integral to the agricultural process. Starvation, disease and inscrutable government policies (Pol Pot had all the male oxen castrated in the Pursat province) had reduced Kampuchean draft animals to one-fourth the number they had the previous decade. (With much of the male population also decimated, the acute labor shortage heightened the difficulty of planting the country's rice land.) Since each draft animal is theoretically capable of tilling enough land to produce 8.5 metric tons of rice (which would feed 500 people annually), replenishing the draft animal population of Kampuchea also became a logical relief priority.

Such draft animals— and ox carts abandoned behind many farm houses— could be easily purchased in Thailand, which had modernized and introduced many small tractors in recent years to till its rice fields. A refugee cart fleet was being assembled. Khmer carpenter-refugees could do necessary repairs on these secondhand carts to ready them for the trip to Kampuchea— thus the need to set up a carpenter's shop within the cordoned area. The vaccination program was aimed at strengthening the draft animals returning to Kampuchea. The "veterinary hospital" was a plot of land allotted by the director of Nong Chan just inside the camp— by the typical Oriental welcoming arch. The soggy ground had been filled with dirt to allow this staging area to remain dry enough so that the carts and animals could be worked on there.

Greg, another Phnom Penh-headed relief worker with the Heifer Project, was on his first trip to the refugee camp, yet was already placed in charge of the vet hospital. He planned to vaccinate, deworm and treat the animals passing through the land bridge. A citizen of the world, Greg was born and educated in New Zealand, had worked in Japan and England and had come to Thailand from six years in a cat-and-dog practice in Brooklyn. He had brought 1,600 doses of rinderpest vaccine out to the border which needed to be refrigerated— a challenge in this land without electricity. He also had plenty of worm medicine and the basic equipment needed to start treating foot rot— an especially debilitating infection which was always aggravated by the monsoon season.

Captain Tiradaet had told us we had to observe the 8 PM curfew, so we left Nong Chan around six, deciding that we should celebrate and eat out on the town. Never have I done this so literally.

Downtown Koke Sung consisted of only two establishments—a general store and the open-air eating place (restaurant would be strictly euphemistic) where we were eating out. A roof and two walls enclosed a dirt-floored open space which held four tables "inside", while there were three tables outside on the "curb". For a counter, there was a rickety wood table and two aluminum basins used as sinks. A primitive butane stove and a glass-enclosed case displaying peeled onions, garlic, boiled eggs and baby cucumbers—the condiments necessary for a tasty Thai meal—completed their equipment.

We had stopped by the house in Koke Sung to pick up the truck driver who had been supervising the local crew which was getting the cart repair shop in operation and the cattle and oxcart buyer. So our party of seven made the pretty proprietress look happy as she greeted us in the customary Thai manner— praying hands held to the middle of the eyes while making a slight bow. I asked her where I could wash my hands and she led me out back where two girls seated on low stools scrubbed and pared vegetables. The proprietress gave me a piece of soap and one of the girls got up to hold a jar of water and pour it over my hands when I was ready to rinse.

While I was gone everyone had settled in at two tables outside— it was still hot and muggy so even the hint of a breeze was welcome. Our table was separated from the road by a ditch filled with stagnant, muddy water and intermittent plank bridges. I was nicely settled trying to absorb my surroundings when a dog sniffing for a tidbit along the edge tumbled into the ditch by my feet managing to splash grubby water on my pants in the process.

I was distracted from my irritation by the proprietress who just then began filling the table with small dishes—fish relish, hot mustard and pepper sauces, soy sauce. Then each person was given a large bowl of white rice, a soup spoon and a tinny fork. The main dishes were put in the middle of the table and the proper way to eat was to dish spoonfuls from the common plates into your bowl. Most eating is done with the spoon, but it was OK to shove food onto the spoon with the fork. Greg and John warned me that much of the food was spicy hot. I decided to concentrate on an omelette after tentatively tasting a few of the dishes which left my mouth burning the rest of the evening just from the sample.

Night fell and the warm, humid evening almost seemed tranquil as cicadas began singing in the trees. Periodically they were drowned out by motorcycles, pickup trucks or armored personnel carriers rumbling through on this main thoroughfare—a constant reminder that we were in a war zone.

As we were finishing three Khmer children ambled past the table with broad smiles and began talking to us. One asked in broken Thai if we wanted to live with them. They laughed. We laughed. They then said they were hungry and laughed again. When we offered them some food, they said they were full. Roongroj told us not to worry, he would handle this situation for us.

John asked them their names. Tumrag handled the introductions, telling us his own, then pointing out Bokwun and Chumroen. Tumrag also told John that two months before he had interviewed him—as part of a fact-finding task. All three were from Phnom Penh and all three were orphans. Tumrag looked to me to be about eight years of age, but I knew that sizes of malnourished children can often be deceiving. He didn't know his last name or his age. He told us that Pol Pot had killed his parents before they had told him his name and his age. I asked where they slept. Tumrag again answered, "Wherever I am." Roongroj explained they were children of the temple, which meant they slept at the local wat and ate there.

Roongroj ordered another bowl of rice for the children and then spooned the rest of our main dishes over this. Sitting the children at the next table he watched them divide the bounty.

A half moon was now peeping through cirrus clouds. Only the brighter planets were visible. Greg said, "How I love the nights here! After six years in Brooklyn, I'd forgotten stars even existed!"

It was 7:30 and time to go. Back at the rented house we discovered the Thais had closed all the wooden shutters Greg and I had flung open when we had stopped by earlier to let in every possible wisp of breeze. I explained to Greg that most people in the interior of Brazil say the night air kills you, so I guessed that the Thais probably felt the same way. With malaria prevalent, it's not a bad belief. But we were taking antimalarial drugs and had mosquito netting for sleeping, so we went around reopening the shutters, letting in the sweet, jasmine-laden night air.

Typically a Thai home is an unpartitioned loft built on ten-foot stilts—which makes the houses look somewhat like lake dwellings where someone forgot to put in the lake. Perched on such piles, these homes are built high enough up to catch the prevailing winds that cool the land while providing space underneath for huddling their animals to protect them from monsoon rains and preying animals—with two feet or four. This space below in the Oxfam house would be filled with tools and equipment for the oxcart repair operation.

In most Thai homes a galvanized, brick-lined bucket which burns charcoal stands in one corner of the loft room designating that area as the kitchen. Beyond that there are no chairs, no furniture and usually no table. (It was impressive to observe the Thais' ability to sit on their haunches all day long--obviously a discipline learned from childhood.) Clothes and bedrolls are stored in another corner and since many people wear sarongs—a wrapped-around, handloomed cloth—the wardrobe tends to be simple to manage.

Our house in Koke Sung was more sophisticated than our neighbors' in that it had one corner partitioned off for a private bedroom with walls halfway to the ceiling topped by slats to the roof which allowed for good ventilation. But the neighbors won the Jones-battle insofar as they had a "bathroom" which we did not. This was a lowered porch on the far side of their house with an enclosed corner for the cleanest outdoor toilet I have seen. A tile platform with grooves for your feet was set in the cement floor and a large Chinese-decorated earthen water jar that held about 50 gallons of water with a ladle meant not only could you wash down the toilet, but by standing over another drain in the floor, you had a convenient spot to shower or shave. Until our place had a bathroom added, the neighbors offered to let the refugee workers staying in the house use their facilities.

Everyone takes their shoes off and leaves them at the bottom of the stairs when entering a Thai house, so floors stay remarkably clean. Most Thai bathe two or three times a day—not only because they are a very clean people but because it is a grand cooling technique. Many bathe at the decorated earthen water jars which stand under the eaves of each Thai house to collect rain water from their corrugated tin roofs through movable spouts which are placed over one jar and then the next as they fill. The Thais bathe leaving their sarongs on, soaping themselves, then dishing water out of the jar to rinse off. All very handy. The men tie their sarongs around their waists, the women tie them higher—although it is acceptable for very old women and very young girls to tie theirs at the waist. As the sarongs dry they cool the body. There are many ways to create your own private refrigeration, I've discovered!

The most unwieldy item we had brought to the border had been the kerosene refrigerator. The Thais had unloaded it from the truck, but hadn't known where we would want to put such an odd item. John and Greg decided it needed to be kept inside the house because of the vaccines. With everyone helping by word or deed, the refrigerator finally made it up the narrow stairs on the outside of the house and into a corner. By Thai standards our house looked overstocked because we also had a table.

The refrigerator was identical to one I had in Brazil for eleven years. John filled it with kerosene and then lit it. Its wick began burning blue, and I knew it would soon be cold, so Greg and I began filling it with vaccines from the ice chest. The only food we added were three high-energy biscuits Greg had brought from the States—"compressed cat food" as he called them.

Greg and John had done all the purchasing for the house— buying mattresses, pillows, sheets and mosquito netting as well as a truck full of carpenter's tools, rods for axletrees and leaves for springs. But they had completely forgotten any amenities—no cleaning materials, no soap, no towels. I was too Western on the inside to feel that you could take a bath and just dry off in the air, so I was glad that I'd brought my own towel. John and Greg joined our neighbors and the Oxfam workers who were sitting on their haunches under the house enjoying the night breezes while I got our solitary towel and went next door to try out our neighbors' bathroom.

I left everyone discussing the day and the events and the questions in the air: what would the Vietnamese do now that the Thai government had three days ago begun the repatriation—sending refugees back to Kampuchea? The Vietnamese had warned that they viewed this as an aggressive act because many of those going back were Khmer Rouge/Pol Pot soldiers—now fed and rehabilitated and ready to launch the monsoon offensive against the Heng Samrin government. Monsoons are for guerrillas.

In these complicated matters the consensus seemed to be: There are no such things as clean decisions or right and wrong answers. What left me incredulous was that the American government, in its current Russophobia, not only was still recognizing and supporting the fallen Pol Pot regime but was reputedly providing the Pol Pot guerrillas with supplies and was pushing the repatriation move. And Pol Pot had never even suggested that he was changing his spots or was even sorry for the mayhem.

One of my first evenings in Bangkok I had dined with a French journalist, Marcel, who had just returned from an escorted tour to the Pol Pot hideaway inside Kampuchea. Marcel was amazed because even with foreign journalists the Pol Pot people were not admitting that the Khmer Rouge had made any basic policy errors while in office. Sure, they said, excesses had occurred, but Marcel perceived them as intransigent and in fact planning to reinstate their same program when they got back in power.

(Having heard so many anti-Communist declarations from the American press, it was hard for me to understand what rationale America continued to use to back the Pol Pot—the worst Communist government ever instituted. But humiliated and defeated by the Vietnamese, it appeared we had no scruples in choosing any bedfellows to continue this war against them.)

John's consternation at what was happening was based on history: The year before a similar repatriation had sent 60,000 Khmers back to Kampuchea in two days. Between land mines, natural disasters and enemy forces, it is estimated that half these people were dead within 48 hours. The UNHCR was also upset because coercion by the Pol Pot elements in the refugee camps was being placed on the Khmers to return. A ditty being sung said, "Those who return first will sleep on beds; those who return second will sleep on cots; those who return next will sleep on the ground; and those who return last will sleep under the ground." Relief workers and UNHCR representatives were interviewing all those returning to Kampuchea to make sure their rights were being protected, but there was a lot of unease about the operation.

The Vietnamese attitude was also understandable: since the Khmer Rouge's debilitated forces had sought refuge the year before in Thailand where they had been fed and succored and apparently rearmed—according to intelligence reports—to allow these fighting forces to return to Kampuchea was asking for added mayhem. The land bridge could very well be closed if the Vietnamese saw it as a funnel for rehabilitated guerrilla fighters, so that the food, seed and relief could no longer enter Kampuchea by land.

By the time I had showered and bowed, thanking my neighbors for their hospitality, John was in a sarong looking pretty native. He had bathed at the pots along with the Thais. Everything was quieting. Some unspoken agreement made all our Thai associates retreat to separate digs. I wondered if my presence was the determining factor, but no one said anything.

Greg and I strung up the mosquito netting around the three mattresses lying on the floor. Then I sat on the floor, against a wall next to a kerosene lamp, jotting notes, but the mosquitos started biting. Even with my antimalarial pills, I still didn't relish the thought of tempting my luck, so decided to crawl under my net. Though it wasn't yet nine, it seemed to all of us that going to bed was the sensible way to escape those mosquitos.

John locked the door and said good night. Greg responded but soon his regular breathing told the tale. I started to squirrel myself into my one sheet. For some reason my long limbs always leave my feet cold, no matter the tropics, and I knew I needed them covered. I made a cocoon and settled into my pillow. The night sounds were beginning to be comfortable when a distant explosion sounded. Greg slept on but John and I both started.

"What was that?"

"I don't know. Possibly a land mine."

Then I remembered I had forgotten my evening prayers. I began them silently and added the safety of those whose lives were endangered. Still I couldn't sleep. The quick staccato of fire-crackers which I knew were not for any Independence Day celebration sounded and I found myself praying for the comfort of any who might be victims to this menance.

Another hollow boom sounded. In the dark, John spoke up, "This village has never been mortared." It seemed hollow comfort. He added, "They've fallen on both sides of Koke Sung, but never here."

My prayers became slightly fervent and I remembered to ask after my guardian angels. John's breathing deepened. I went to sleep asking my question, "When will justice and peace reign on the earth?"

By the time I was up, teeth brushed, hair combed and putting on some fresh clothes, I found my watch: 5:30! The morning noises had begun quite a while before: geese honking across the street, cows and chickens corralled under the house next door announcing the day, trucks and motorcycles roaring down the thoroughfare in front. The fresh morning crispness and the glorious sunrise were filling the sky with rose-streaked clouds. The palm trees silhouetted black against the horizon were being painted in technicolor. Night is the winter of the tropics and you wake forgetting the heat that is sure to follow. What I could not forget were the night noises.

Roongroj appeared with breakfast—a pot of freshly cooked rice, dried fish and a concoction of squash, red peppers and sardines. We all sat on the front porch, on the floor. In Thailand you must be careful about your feet. Since they are the lowest member of the body, it is degrading to point them at anyone. I tried to sit cross-legged with my feet tucked properly underneath me, out of sight, but my ankles started to hurt. I finally turned so they would only point at Greg who assured me he didn't mind.

It was too early for my stomach to cope, so I settled for cafe au lait. John produced some sweetened condensed milk manufactured by a Swiss transnational corporation. The can had bold instructions on the label in Thai and English claiming it was suitable for infants. You could not escape the many who were willing to violate the World Health Organization's guidelines to establish a profitable market.

By 7:30 we were headed back to Nong Chan. Halfway to the refugee camp we came upon over a hundred people running down the road towards the camp. John pointed out that Tiradaet and his troops had just driven up to an open Thai roadside market. Although this marketing was illegal, the Thais brought their products and the refugees walked from the camp to purchase them. Every now and then the soldiers would confiscate someone's goods, but mostly the soldiers survived by taking their cut from the operation. John noted that Tiradaet was driving a new pickup truck. At one of the checkpoints there were about 20 such seized from various smugglers and held for several months—providing a convenient source of transportation to the border patrol.

I began to think about the Thais who get rich off refugees and Swiss companies who get rich off ignorant and poor lactating mothers in the Third World. Really all in the same class. Fortunately these are balanced with the kind, generous Thais who assist John in the relief project and with companies that eschew merciless exploitation. But in the final analysis, justice is everyone's concern.

As we drove the last mile into camp we must have passed a thousand people coming home from the market carrying pineapples, garlic, tropical fruits I couldn't identify, pop, beer, eggs, dried fish and the omnipresent small, red-hot peppers. These were what made life worth living in the row upon dull row of thatched shacks and the empty, toilless life.

The couple of thousand refugees who walked the mile to market and back often came back to sell their wares to the other thousands back home. The camp roads were lined with vendors who squatted behind goods placed on a cloth on the ground. Cigarettes were sold singly or by the pack, depending on your wealth. As we were parking the van, John said, "Hey, look at the French bread—that's a real rarity here in Thailand. We should get some!"

Greg and I exchanged glances. There were flies swarming all over it. "Well, I guess it's pretty exposed to the elements," John said, relieving us loads. There is a point beyond which going native is a loss of sagacity.

But John was elated. The jungle telegraph had worked again and Virat had already turned out about 60 water buffalo and oxen which were standing patiently tied to the bamboo fence in the staging area. Virat, who has a withered arm, was on a small knoll with a bullhorn in his good hand directing traffic. He was certainly showing his organizational abilities that day, and I knew why he was part of the Khmer camp leadership.

Greg and John began setting up for the operation—mixing vaccines from the ice chest in the back of the van, preparing the worm medicine applicators, getting the ropes out. The crowds moved in on John and Greg, watching their every step.

After the first animal tried valiantly to break both Greg's legs in exchange for being vaccinated, they rigged up an ingenious chute. Obviously these Khmers had built similar portable corrals before. Underneath a large, shady tree they made a makeshift corral out of ropes attached to the tree plus two sturdy branches used to form a wedge. Two Khmers pressed the branches against the draft animal as the owner led it into the wedge. While the victim was caught against the tree, John applied worm medicine through the mouth, Greg gave the vaccine shot in the flank, and Virat sprayed a spot of red paint on the forehead in lieu of tattooing. The wedge opened and the animal was backed out before it really became cognizant what all the confusion was about. The operation became so efficient that they were moving animals through every 15 seconds.

Greg was tremendously impressed with the Khmers' ability to manage animals and said they were some of the best he had ever seen. There were exceptions. One water buffalo walked right through the wedge charging John. Fortunately he was quick to jump and so only had a bruised arm and a torn sleeve for a souvenir.

After my 15 years on a ranch in the interior of Brazil I had no fascination in joining the vaccination process. My theory is that there is always someone who likes doing what I find distasteful, so I contribute to the enjoyment economy of the world by letting them do it. Besides I wanted to write in my journal and take some more pictures and remember all the truth I was incarnating.

Finding a comfortable spot where I could write that was shady and breezy was hard. My Norwegian heritage, I long ago decided, has left me genetically unprepared for heat. Peng came to my rescue and backed the van into the shade. By sitting with the side door open, I could catch the breeze.

Immediately children began to press in. Where four stopped to look, 40 gathered. The door held a stair step of little bodies, medium-sized bodies and the larger ones standing behind, all staring, all inching forward. They were so close I could feel their breath on my arm. Periodically Peng would walk around the van, pushing everyone back, nervous that they might touch something. But when you have nothing to do, a stranger doing anything is worth the same attention as John Wayne on the late, late.

Without understanding a word, I knew they were commenting on my calligraphy, my language and my personhood. Again I felt that strange deafness. What struck me was how these Khmer smelled like frontier Brazilians. It must come from drying clothes and standing over open fires, or from bathing in basins. Or perhaps all jungles smell alike!

I wandered back to kibitz the vets and get some fresh air. By the time I got back to the van Peng had almost departed this vale. That morning when we loaded the van, Greg had warned us in English not to confuse the plastic bottle of Formalin—a strong, but clear disinfectant to be used on the foot rot patients— with the water jug. Peng had done just that, but fortunately had not swallowed. But he used up the gallon of water we had along rinsing out his mouth.

Roongroj solved our problem of having no potable water left by appearing shortly with some pop which he had scavanged somewhere in the camp. I helped him put it in the ice chest with the vaccines. He also produced a lone glass and gave it to me. I could tell from Roongroj's attitude toward that glass that a lady was expected to drink out of a glass, not a bottle.

After a bit Roongroj and Peng took off with the van to get supplies and bring our lunch. Just before they returned, another buffalo charged through the corral, smashing it. It was time for a break. Roongroj showed up with a dozen little plastic sacks filled with fried rice. What an efficient picnic! Everybody participating in the operation was given a ration and a Chinese soup spoon. To top it off someone pulled a watermelon out of the van. A great lunch, altogether!

After lunch I somehow needed to get away from all these people. I eyed the nearby watchtower, remembering my great two-storied tree house in Brazil. John assured me I could go up. Constructed of tall bamboo posts, it also had two stories. I climbed past two blue-uniformed guards on the first platform who did not stir from their afternoon siesta. The guard on the second level woke, sat up, but said nothing. Apparently strange Western women were expected to wander around, so I decided to sit down as if I belonged there. There were two bamboo benches on the top deck which made it easier for my Western limbs and I sat facing the guard on the opposite bench.

It was delightful. No flies, no pressing bodies, breezy because it was high up into the prevailing wind currents. I could see the entire camp and beyond into the Kampuchea jungle area which ringed the pocket of the camp. The wind picked up and I realized how rickety the tower was, but then Thai houses shake whenever any-one walks across the floor so I presume you get used to the swaying.

The red UNICEF tank trucks conveying potable water for 50,000 people kept rumbling by, brightening up the scene. Long lines of trucks filled the myriad water boxes where children and young girls came with buckets balanced on long poles. One man in a cart was filling up a dozen cans— probably to carry to the far end of the camp. It was a formidable task trying to ferry in sufficient drinking water.

Even up here I could hear the steady stream of sandal-slapping feet as hundreds of pedestrians passed by on the road. Frequently motorbikes and motorcycles roared past. The vehicles tended to belong to aid agencies. Only the bicycles passed silently.

Most of the dark-skinned Khmers in this camp wore the traditional sarongs. Women wore them ankle-length, men at the calf. Everyone seemed to have a long, plaid scarf tied around some part of the body— convenient for wiping off humidity and available for wrap-ping when the breezes came up or when it started to rain. John had his scarf around his waist— on top of his button-down oxford cloth shirt and cord pants. Later when we got caught in a rain storm he used his tied around his head to keep the rain out of his eyes.

When I had jotted my notes and filled up my solitude cracks, I descended once again to the world out there. I knew if I were brave

I would go down the tilted ladders frontwards, but at my age prudence being the better part, I backed down cautiously.

Robert Ashe, Red Cross director for Nong Chan, was watching the cattle operation when I got back. The 26-year-old son of a prominent Anglican priest, he had earlier that month been named a Member of the British Empire (MBE) on Queen Elizabeth II's birthday honors list for his humanitarian work with the refugees.

I asked Robert about the explosions the night before. They were B-40 rockets, he explained in a matter-of-fact manner. The Khmer Seri who controlled Nong Chan had captured four Vietnamese in the fire fight. One Vietnamese soldier had been wounded, but had died before noon.

Robert was another quiet soul. He said that satellite intelligence reported 15,000 Vietnamese soldiers were headed straight for Nong Chan and would probably reach the camp by midnight. When I asked what the people in the camp were doing, he resignedly shrugged his shoulders. In the face of imminent attack, the non-violent and the unarmed have few options.

By now Greg had taught several of the Khmer and Thai how to vaccinate so the process was speeded up. My enjoyment theory held. And both Greg and John were elated. By one o'clock they had already exhausted the worm medicine, vaccinated 216 head for rinderpest and treated many foot rot cases. Greg said, "I'll tell you one thing, this is the busiest practice I've ever seen!"

We decided to take a break and go to the back half of the camp again. The van drove us to the end of the road where we began trekking. John pointed out a new signboard outside the hospital and feeding station where the pictures of a couple hundred children were posted. They apparently were orphans, but these pictures were being circulated throughout all the refugee camps in the hopes that someone could identify them or claim some relationship before they became officially regarded as orphans. I thought of our three young temple dwellers from last night's dinner.

A Khmer intercepted our walkthrough, handing John a sheaf of translated interviews. John had been surveying the point of origin for the various refugee families and also had asked all newly-arriving families about the conditions of the rice planting at home, the number of draft animals available and the agricultural implements extant. He was trying to bring some order to the chaos of food and farm implement distribution.

As part of the repatriation drive, the Red Cross had not

distributed any relief food for a week, hoping to force some of the 50,000 people to return to Kampuchea. As we climbed a knoll, we came upon a half dozen people threshing out seed rice—poles pounding the grain in bowl-shaped holes. They obviously were going to hang on here rather than join those going back and were willing to eat the rice seed they had collected to take back home.

I gazed across to the Kampuchean jungle. It appeared so benign, but how many gruesome memories did it harbor? A wind came up and the sky was darkening. I remembered those clouds from the Brazilian jungles and told Greg and John, "In ten minutes we are going to get a storm here!"

They looked up and agreed, so we started back to the van, only to find it gone. Peng must have gone on an errand and John said he would go look for him. In a few minutes some great plops of rain began to fall, and I decided it was foolish to just stand there. I told Greg and Kumjorn, "I'm running for it!" and took off.

My OK-OK children laughed gleefully to see me jogging down the road to the front of the camp. They started jogging alongside, cheerily urging me on with our only communication system, "OK! OK!" The gale was wildly blustering the blue plastic roofs away and the Khmers were frantically clutching and holding, trying to keep them intact so they would have some protection left when the rain began to pour. I knew—as they did—that the wind was at the inter-face of the two fronts and would die down as soon as the rain started pouring seriously.

Finally a Land Rover came down the road and John and a driver stopped and asked if I wanted to ride back. It sure beat standing in the rain, so I hopped in. By the time we had caught up to Greg and Kumjorn the rain was pelting in through John's window which wouldn't shut. Our van appeared behind us and the soupy road was miring it down. Greg said, "We'll never get out of here now!"

I assured him there was no problem. My expertise in assaying mud conditions was hard-earned knowledge. By now we were five in the Land Rover and getting stuck. John said, "Everybody out," but when I started out the door Kumjorn and the driver indicated that I should stay in. My feminism only travels so far! I stayed.

But I called out to John, "You need to get people to stand on the back axle of the van so it can get traction and climb that hill." John, Greg and Kumjorn by now were sopped and here I was straining our community by giving dry advice. I sat back and pulled out my Chinese fan—it felt even hotter! The steamy jungle rain doesn't allow any cooling evaporation to happen. Soon the van was unstuck, thanks to the drenched souls who stood on the back bumper providing the automatic rear wheel drive, and we headed for the gate.

Obviously our cattle operation was over for the day and we headed back to Koke Sung to pack up. Greg and John decided we needed to head back to Bangkok for more supplies. They were still dripping wet, but decided not to change, so quickly we settled into the car for the ride back. Peng flung us down the road towards civilization— a tired, hot and quiet lot.

The next morning with ease I again accepted showers and electricity and the comforts as my due. At breakfast I read the English-language paper and was horror-struck: nine hours after we left Koke Sung the Vietnamese had invaded Nong Chan. I called John and found the news was even more harrowing than I anticipated: Koke Sung's luck had changed. In the early morning hours a mortar fell behind the house where we had slept that previous night blowing out the brains of a seven-year-old boy who had been scampering around our feet the day before. Captain Tiradaet Muengaew made the paper. He had led a counterattack on the Vietnamese and was almost immediately cut down along with all 16 of his men.

I sat that day overlooking the Bay of Thailand wondering where Granny Morn was. John said that the 50,000 refugees were fleeing through adjacent rice paddies, cowering as the artillery fire from both sides arched overhead. Those cavorting OK-OK children were once again on the edge of a precipice.

The Oxfam employees had locked the door to the newly-rented house, piled themselves into the truck and helped the hamlet to evacuate. I worried about the vaccine. The kerosene would run out in a few days and there were 1,200 specially imported doses left!

Four days later the Vietnamese captured Robert Ashe and three other Westerners as they were searching Nong Chan for possible wounded. The land bridge was closed. The 50,000 Nong Chan refugees were being placed in the other burgeoning camps further inside the border.

A week later I was back in the States and found that the draft registration vote had passed. I kept wondering how many Captain Tiradaets I was going to be meeting. The only bright spot was the news that Robert and his companions had been released and a note from John saying the vaccine was fine. Roongroj and Peng had gone back to Koke Sung and filled the refrigerator. He and Greg were going full speed ahead with the Oxbridge Project trusting that the way would soon be open for them to send the oxcarts and draft animals into Kampuchea. I decided to put the land bridge on my prayer list.

But still I am asking my question that never gets answered, "When will peace and justice reign on this earth?"

Chapter _____ 7

A Colombian Odyssey

After several years in big city life, I was glad to take an assignment that led me back to the jungles. I knew what to expect as far as the terrain was concerned and had heard about Bruce Olson's rather remarkable undertaking with the reputedly-fierce Motilone tribe in the jungles of northern Colombia. It would be interesting to see his work up close.

It turned out Bruce wasn't all that easy to find. I had written him from California in October telling him who I was and what I wanted and had said I was hoping to visit him in the next few months. Nothing.

During December I was firming up plans for a trip to Brazil right after New Year's, but still no word from Bruce. Stopping in Colombia on the way seemed the logical plan of action, but I didn't know exactly where to stop. I knew those jungles go on forever! Finally I got a lead from a pastor in the States who contributed to Bruce's work. He had a few telephone numbers in Colombia where Bruce could be reached in case of an emergency. But the pastor admitted

that since Bruce spends much of his time away from any communication device—even with satellites and microwaves making
it possible to talk to virtually every corner or the world now—he
had never been able to locate Bruce at any of these numbers. Rather
he suggested that if I was going to be in the area, my best bet might
be to drop in and try to find him personally.

A missionary friend who went quarterly to Colombia on mission
business agreed to go with me so I wouldn't have to face the jungles
alone. Our rendezvous point turned out to be Medellin—the city
in northern Colombia where I had lived for three years as a child. I
wondered how much I would remember and whether I would find
anyone who had known me during those years.

My plane made a strange, yet proficient, S-approach to the airport around a slight hill smack in the middle of the flight path into
this tropical valley. The baggage carriers were less efficient—
somehow my luggage had been left in Panama, but not to worry—
they would come on the next plane in three days. And so I was
given the luxury of time to find my roots. It was strange seeing all
the shrunken houses, streams and hills of my childhood. I kept
asking missionaries about Maruja Marin—the tall beautiful neighbor
woman who had been my special friend for the years I was in
Colombia. Most of my memories of the years there centered on
adventures with Maruja—a childless woman who had taken time
to show me that world. Besides teaching me the rudiments of
making the local corn bread—plump tortilla patties—she had
spent hours telling me stories or inventing adventurous hikes and
picnics into the hills surrounding that serene valley.

Maruja's husband, Enrique, was a famous sculptor who was
remembered in the community. He had died a few years before,
and someone knew where his widow was living. None of my
recollections of Maruja matched the tiny, old lady who barely
reached my shoulders. She now lived with her niece just a block
from the seminary where my father had taught. But it *felt* like Maruja.
We hugged and laughed about the disparity in our sizes and I
listened to her reminiscing about having strange American neighbors who had taught her some new things, but had also learned
from Maruja important lessons about living in Colombia.

Again we walked up the mountainside together and she got
permission to take me inside from the elderly, cassocked priest
who now rented our old home. He was about to say morning mass
for seven or eight women gathered on the porch where I had

played many an hour. Maruja explained who I was to a few old-timers. Some smiled and nodded recognition.

We wandered around that strange/familiar house and I tried to remember.

"This was your bedroom."

It came back a little but somehow everything was out of synch. Even the tangerine tree where I had often hidden to play with my dolls was diminutive compared to what I recollected.

I wanted to leave before any more memories were shattered. We went next door, but now Maruja refused to go in— she didn't want to return to the home which had given her so many happy remembrances, but she urged me to knock and talk to the people who had bought the home. The door was open so I could see Enrique's murals painted inside on the living room wall. But I couldn't knock and turned away with nothing to say.

Suddenly I spotted it, stooped down and ran my finger down the spine of the touch-sensitive mimosa which still grew alongside the old cobblestoned mountain path— it was gratifying that this childhood memory had not diminished. I ran my finger down several spines and Maruja laughed— I was warmed that she still understood. The thought struck me that perhaps the reason we had done so well at six and 30 was that we were very much alike even then. It certainly seemed as if we responded to life similarly at 40 and 64! I was happy my odyssey had brought me back to Medellin.

The jungle afternoon was filled with normal noises— cicadas were beginning to announce that evening wasn't far off, birds were singing then sweeping over the river in pursuit of fish which surfaced to grab lazy flies which came within reach. The monkeys were out of sight, but you could hear them chattering in the tall trees just beyond the clearing. The changing of the guard was definitely under way— the diurnal crew was making way so the nocturnal gang could set up shop.

The idyllic quiet was interrupted by the putt-putt of a motor— obviously a boat coming upstream. I turned to Jairo, our 15-year-old Motilone guide and asked, "Does that sound like the Iquiacarora boat?" He thought it did. We were over an hour downstream still from Iquiacarora, a large Motilone settlement which boasted a clinic, a schoolhouse and was reputedly to be Bruce's next stop on his itinerary. The Iquiacarora boat had gone downriver to fetch Bruce at the place where the trail coming down from the mountain valleys reached the River of Gold, and we were hoping to intercept it as it went past us upriver.

I hurried down to the river landing and watched the long dugout canoe round the bend and get larger on the horizon. As it got closer I saw one blond head seated amidst a dozen black-haired people. I waved and called out as the boat came even with the landing and the Motilone pilot deftly turned the canoe towards shore.

It had turned out that what was needed to find Bruce Olson was persistence. After flying out of Medellin— again on that S-shaped trajectory— over the Andes peaks to Cucuta, a town on the Venezuelan border, we had squeezed onto one of those cramped buses where the suitcases are loaded on top while the pigs and chickens come inside with their owners. After five hours of bumping over washboard roads, we arrived in Tibu, an oil town whose dusty streets are slicked down with a refinery byproduct which keeps the dust from flying but makes every step a trifle precarious.

Bruce's three phone numbers I had been given turned out were all for different towns. During the wait for my bags in Medellin, I kept trying to call these numbers. The only phone which anyone answered was here in Tibu, but it had done little good. I kept finding myself talking to a woman who only spoke Motilone. Every time I said "Bruce Olson" she would excitedly repeat, "Bruchko" and then carry on at happy length. Perhaps we would do better with sign language than we had managed with my Spanish and her Motilone. I decided to head for Tibu.

I knew from my research that in Tibu the Motilone maintain a large house where any tribal member can stay while being treated at the oil company's hospital. I found out later that the other two telephones had been for houses where Motilone students stayed during the school term. Since January is a vacation month in most of South America, the students were all back home with their tribes.

In Tibu everyone I asked knew about the *Casa Indigena* and pointed us on our way. At the gate of a large stucco home with well-kept lawns, I clapped— the proper way to knock in Latin American jungles I knew— and my telephonist came to the gate. I would recognize her voice anywhere! About five feet tall, she was sturdily built, had jet black hair with straight-cut bangs, a happy face and inquisitive eyes. She held a baby in her arms; another child was holding firmly to her skirt.

Here we go! I thought. At my Spanish query, she nodded, smiled broadly and then went to call Jairo, a bilingual high school student who had just arrived a few hours before from the jungle. It was a relief to find that Jairo not only spoke good Spanish, but also knew Bruce's itinerary for the upcoming days. And best of all, he was willing to go right back to the jungles and guide us in to where he thought we could meet up with Bruce. He had heard Bruce ask the Iquiacarora boat to meet him and knew that he was scheduled the following day to pass a certain point in the river which wouldn't be too difficult for us to reach. Bruce was in the middle of making his circuit run—visiting the villages, tending to the sick, finding out how things were going.

Jairo explained that the pickup we needed for the next leg of the trip only made one trip a day—leaving Tibu at 6 AM, arriving at the end of the road, downstream from where we needed to go, at 10:30 AM. The next morning we crowded into the bed of a '42 Ford pickup which had two planks down each side for first-class seating. Unlucky coach-class passengers hung on behind or dangled off the running board.

The road followed the oil pipeline as it went into the interior in a pretty straight line—but up and down very hilly terrain. Although the Andes peaks were nowhere in sight, it was easy to see that we were on the tropical foothills that led up to them. After a breezy and bumpy early morning ride we came to the village of Pista on the River of Gold (named by some hopeful explorer).

In Pista we could find no one who wanted to take us upriver to our rendezvous point. Since in the previous five years the rainfall had diminished 60 inches per year, the river was so low that going upstream from Pista was precarious for anyone who didn't have an intimate knowledge of the shallows—a rock could easily sheer off a propeller making it a very expensive and frustrating trip.

Finally Jairo convinced a Colombian from the village, Manolo, who owned a dugout canoe powered by an outboard motor but who knew the river well, to take us upriver for the same amount of money as it had cost us to fly over the Andes from Medellin to Cucuta. Manolo knew he had no competition and was using capitalistic practices at their best!

When we went down to the boat there was nothing inside it—not even thwarts to sit on. I asked Jairo incredulously if we were expected to sit on the gunwhales for 2½ hours. Jairo conferred with Manolo who went back to his house and got two aluminum folding chairs which he carefully placed in the bottom of the dugout. I had to laugh—I somehow felt like Katharine Hepburn in *The African Queen*.

The trip was an unforgettable experience. We passed through beautiful, pristine territory where exotic birds watched us from the tops of gigantic jungle trees. Periodically our very shallow draft was still too much, so Manolo had us climb out of the canoe and walk alongside in the river, shoes and all, to keep the boat from scraping the rocks. The water was crystal clear and we could see fish laze by. I kept worrying about the abrupt climatic change that would drop the rainfall 60 inches in a year and speculated that with the prevailing winds from the east, this was probably another fallout from the devastating denudation of the Amazon's timber that has been going on for the past decade which some ecologists are blaming for drastically unbalancing our earth's ecosystem.

Finally we reached the spot on the river to which Jairo had bargained with Manolo to take us. It struck me that trusting God was the only thing I could do at this point— we were in an unknown jungle, and soon our only link to the outside world was turning around and going downstream. Jairo explained that this river landing belonged to the home of a Motilone, Odo, who had married a Colombian and was living on the edge of the Motilone's territory— halfway between his world and hers. We were to wait there and see how accurate the jungle telegraph really was.

An hour later when Bruce stepped out of the dugout, and extended his hand, I felt like saying, "Dr. Livingstone, I presume?" But I didn't know then whether or not he had a sense of humor. In any case I felt like an accomplished scout having flushed him out of his jungle habitat— and also felt like I should sing the doxology.

The disparity between Bruce's tall Nordic frame and the short, stocky Motilone was the first thing I noticed. Yet his ease in communicating with them and their naturalness with him somehow made him fit into their world, making him almost feel foreign to me.

At one point I commented, "You seem very much like a Motilone in many ways."

"Yes, even though I know that I will never be a Motilone and will always be different from them, yet at the same time I will never again be fully comfortable in the culture where I was raised."

I could relate to this dichotomy after having spent 18 years in Latin America. To become a missionary or a cross-cultural person is to give up not only the homeland, but also the sense of belonging in that homeland. Yet I could envy Bruce his enculturating experience with the Motilone who are certainly an admirable people.

Calm, soft-spoken and curious, they are gentle with their children, generous and obviously content with what most Americans would call a rather primitive existence.

Bruce had taken on many of these Motilone characteristics in two decades of living with them, and I had come all this way into the jungle to see for myself what he had been able to accomplish among this tribe. Some anthropologists were especially commending his success in preserving the traditional Motilone life-style while helping them make a rather traumatic, yet necessary, transition into the modern age.

After that first meeting we talked for nine hours nonstop. Through supper which the wife of our Motilone host insisted on preparing for everyone, through another hour's boat ride further upriver to Iquiacarora, and then while sitting in front of the clinic watching the full moon make its way across the sky, he told us his story of how he had come to work with the Motilone tribe.

So that we might get a better feel for the Motilone and their world, Bruce invited us to accompany him for the next few days as he made his rounds. Walking down the jungle trails where exotic vines dangle and thousands of varieties of orchids and flowers paint a serene picture, I found the loud cries of various tropical birds and screeching monkeys somehow discordant. I knew they were protesting our invasion of their particular turf and were also advising their neighbors of the intruders. Our presence was obviously disturbing the local peace. But since power and might also rule the jungle, these small creatures could only protest stridently.

As I waded through the streams and squished along the muddy trail behind our Motilone guides going ever deeper into their traditional land which straddles the Colombian/Venezuelan border, I reflected on how these indigenous people live in amazing harmony with their environment, understanding their tropical homeland.

Then the analogy struck me of how the Motilone life-style resembles that of the animals and birds who live in their area. For the past 450 years the Motilone, like the animals, have been a territorial people. Following the laws of the jungle they have used all their might and power to keep foreigners off their turf.

Spanish conquistadores, hearing or dreaming of fabulous gold mines, built a road through Motilone territory in the 16th century, establishing a settlement as a local power base in their valley. The extant ruins of the Spanish chapel are a silent witness of the cross which accompanied the sword into the New World and acquiesced in the plundering of the gold and precious metals which belonged to indigenous peoples. Spanish and European churches are still filled with gold objects sacked from the pacific peoples of Latin America.

That the Motilone refused to be plundered is a testimony to their own feelings of self-worth, and down through the centuries they have become feared as dreaded cannibals who killed all who ventured onto their territory. The murderous and unscrupulous Spaniards who settled in the Catacumba River Valley—which funnels water from the Andes down to oil-rich Lake Maracaibo—never made it back to Spain. They were massacred as they trekked their way back to the coast and the Old World.

The jungle growth of the last four centuries has since swallowed up the gold bullion which they dropped. But the lesson of the Spanish invaders was never forgotten by the Motilone who knew that no peaceful coexistence was possible with these foreigners whose intentions were not altruistic. So to the Motilone the white tribe became known as cannibals, and they established a tradition and subsequently killed everyone from that murderous and stealing race who invaded their turf.

Until Bruce Olson. It still isn't clear to them why they allowed this young Minnesotan to live. The Motilone shot him in the leg with a poisoned arrow when he first ventured on their territory, but the tall, gangly blond youth with a gentle face and a backpack who felt called of God to minister to these people must not have looked like a normal oil prospector or a Colombian land poacher. Fortunately Bruce had a strong body which didn't succumb to the fever and infection which set in from his leg wound. So rather miraculously he did survive, although it was almost a year before he emerged from the jungle. When he finally did it was like a resurrection, for most people had assumed he was one more to fall prey to the ferocious Motilone.

Perhaps Bruce survived because it was part of God's providential care of this tribe. They were quickly reaching the end of their ability to fend off the invader and protect themselves. Their homeland was being surrounded by Western oil companies, mineral prospectors and land developers. People in the area recount how Texaco planes firebombed the Motilone longhouses to force them to move off their oil-rich land. Remaining isolated and protected from the greedy outside world was no longer possible.

The Motilone, aside from their reputation, are a people who live at peace in their exotic jungle. In their tribe there is no homicide, drunkenness, prostitution or physical violence. Amongst them there is a true sense of community, of belonging to one another— something which is forever lost to our own individualistic culture. Besides, they truly enjoy life immensely in their habitat. Everything they do is made into a sport: hunting, weaving, fishing, grinding, collecting the earth's produce— all become part of their happy modus vivendi. A daily grind is something they do not know.

One morning Bruce asked us if we wanted to go fishing with the tribal members living at Iquiacarora. The venture started with a 45-minute trek through the jungle to a site chosen on a nearby river. The early birds who had arrived long ahead of us had already enclosed a U-section of the river with a stone dam reinforced with banana leaves. There was some leakage, but this damming process gradually dropped the water level in the U, which in turn exposed the fish trapped inside so that the Motilone men, with long-honed expertise, could proceed to spear these vulnerable fish on thin wooden shafts which they sharpened after each thrust with the knives held in their teeth.

It was a grand party with some 80 men, women and children. The sun sparkled off the wet, finely muscled bodies of the men fishing-- obviously the stars of this show. There was much laughter when someone lost a squirming fish off the end of the spear or made a wrong move and fell into the water. But underneath the gaiety, you knew instinctively that this was also serious competition. After a couple of hours some men had 50 or 60 fish on their vine stringers which they nonchalantly trailed in the cool water, but like fishers the world over, you could feel their contentment at having been successful in their catch.

This also was a great equalizer for the tribe because the bilingual younger folk who were home on vacation from their schools were not doing as well. Somehow their ability to read was mitigated by the fact that they could not spear with the proficiency of those who stayed behind. I tried once to spear a fish, but my heart really wasn't in it, and I could tell my skill needed more than a little upgrading!

The day took on the feeling of a 4th of July picnic. Children were happily grubbing crabs out from under the rocks along the mud banks and the women were collecting broad leaves for wrapping and carrying the fish back home. Everyone knew their role at this party. To complete the celebration, on the trip home (instead of gunnysack races) the men would be lining up along the jungle trail—old men at the front on a handicapped basis—for a foot race back home. The Motilone are a short, but compactly and well-built people and the race was for the prize of winning. (Chieftains in the tribe must be the best hunters, fishers and runners, so all the day's events were important to their status in the community.)

I was feeling really fortunate to have landed at Iquiacarora with such good timing to be able to participate in this fishing festival. Turning to Bruce, I asked how often such a fishing excursion occurred. During the dry season (January to March), he told me, they did this three or four times a week! And then during the rainy season they hunted with the same intensity! My Protestant work ethic marveled at their getting away with making every day into such a holiday lark! What had they done to have God give them such a glorious life? Of course they didn't have paved highways and electric blenders and color TVs, but they certainly seemed content with their lot on this globe.

Late in the afternoon, the party was somewhat marred when a nine-year old boy got too close to someone wielding a knife and was gashed in the leg. He was carried piggyback by a sturdy young warrior to Iquiacacora's clinic where I watched Bruce deftly cleanse the wound, putting nine stiches in the boy's leg.

Bruce's wide-ranging abilities were amazing. I asked, "How do you account for all the varied skills you've managed to acquire without the standard credentialing or even spending time on university campuses?"

"I suppose it was a combination of many factors. The Motilone were willing to accept me and knew that I was here to help. But besides this trust in me, I was also the only one here, so I felt obliged to read and, whenever possible, observe techniques, always asking questions so I could come back here and provide the necessary services. Their need has forced me to develop these skills. Now I can perform many basic medical procedures and I have become a pretty good diagnostician as well. Of course in all of this, I have felt that God has continued to help and guide me."

I had about decided that the Motilone were leading a truly idyllic life. Besides having this liaison with the outside world who was devoted to their well-being, they had an enormous gift of truly enjoying their way of life. Bruce said that the Motilone were also a religious people, concerned with pleasing God.

Their tribal mythology recounts how the knowledge of the trail that led them to God had been lost because of evil ancestors. But not only did they know they had broken communication with their creator, their legends also said that one day a special revelation would come to them which would show them the way to the horizon where their God was to be found. Thus it was easy for many in the tribe to believe Bruce when he began telling them about God's special revelation, Jesus, who had built a bridge that all people could use to once again establish communication with their creator.

Some people consider the Motilone to be a very lucky people. Or perhaps just as Cornelius pleased God through his prayers and his piety so that Peter was sent to share the Good News with this unclean neighbor, they, too, pleased God through their earnest desire to relocate the trail that would lead them to God. And God, who seems to prefer taking the small and foolish ones of this world to confound the wise, led a lanky 19-year-old blond Scandinavian who had no qualifications to attract the attention of established mission organizations (several had turned down his early application summarily), and called him to go to the Motilone.

With the simplicity and trust of the very young, this ingenuous, nascent linguist—Bruce Olson—left college in the middle of his studies to follow a strange urging to go to northern South America and work with indigenous peoples. Having miraculously survived the initial entry, he went on to live among this legendary tribe. Learning their difficult tonal language was a major hurdle, but Bruce's linguistic ability prevailed.

Now, 20 years later, Bruce Olson has also become a legend in his own time. When he first went to South America not only his well-to-do family but also various mission organizations were distressed by his announced intentions to go evangelize the tribal peoples of northern South America. He was assured by them that he had neither the education nor the experience that would prepare him for such an undertaking. When Bruce responded that he knew God was leading him to do this, they were angered by his insolence.

What amazes the mission world today is that while countless missionaries on every continent are being accused of destroying indigenous cultures and making the tribal peoples objects of idle curiosity, someone like Bruce with so little anthropological, theological or cross-cultural training could have done so many things so aptly! Perhaps it was just his lack of preparation which allowed Bruce successfully to enter the Motilone territory without preconceived or traditional ideas of how to go about evangelizing a tribal people. Of necessity he had to be sensitive to the tribe and their culture and sensitive to the leading of the Holy Spirit.

He sees his accomplishments as a fruit of his motives: where most missionaries learn a second language as a functional tool, he learned it as a linguist with a love for languages (by 19 he already spoke Hebrew, Latin, Greek, Norwegian and Swedish—now he speaks 15 languages). Since there were no primers and because the Motilone language is so difficult, for the first two years it took him to learn their language Bruce could only live among the tribe—not jump in with all the answers. During this time he also learned to appreciate the Motilone as a people, and respect their incredible ability of living at peace with what appeared to Bruce's Western eyes as a very hostile environment.

Where many missionaries are accused of coming to their work with a pride in their own technology and knowledge along with feelings of superiority in their understanding of the gospel—ready to show the people something—Bruce was really too young for this when he came. He admits that he has learned as much from the Motilone as they have from him, which rules out any feelings of superiority on his part.

Consequently what he has been able to accomplish—as a catalyst or as an organizer—has been phenomenal. And in the process he has communicated the message of Christ to these indigenous people within the context of their own images and myths, doing it in such a way that the entire tribe—happy to hear of the Messenger who came to earth to show all people the path back to their Creator—made a corporate decision to follow Jesus Christ as a tribe.

In the beginning Bruce did not preach to the entire tribe. Rather he concentrated on communicating the gospel to his pact-brother Bobarishora or Bobby as Bruce came to call him. In this one-on-one evangelization Bruce realized that he had to explain the gospel in Motilone terms which Bobby could understand in his own context.

Thus Bruce told Bobby that in order to find God you had to walk on his trail. Bobby knew that the Motilone mythology said this. But Bruce went on to explain that God's son, Jesus, is the only one who can show us God's trail. In order for that to happen Bobby had to tie his hammock strings into Christ and suspend all his weight on God. This was all in the imagery Bruce had learned from Bobby of how Motilone expressed trust-relationships, for if you trust another person as much as you do the poles to which you secure your hammock 20 feet above the ground, you have entrusted your life to them.

After Bobby made the decision to walk on Jesus' path, he went to a tribal Arrow Festival where he sang to the assembly in their age-old method of relating legends, stories and news of recent events. When he had finished his 14-hour song—in which he had been challenged by another tribal member, but kept answering confident in the veracity of his own song—there occurred what anthropologists term a People Movement. This transpires when an entire people or tribe decide corporately to make a significant ideological change. After Bobby's song, the Motilone decided they wanted Christ to lead them over his bridge to the horizon where God was to be found.

Thus the Motilone were able to find Christ within their own traditional ways. While they preserved their own tribal integrity and mores, they were able to accept a revolutionary new concept. This same pattern has been repeated in other aspects of their life during the last two decades, as they have been confronted with the demands of living in juxtaposition with a modern, technological world.

After spending five fascinating days with the Motilone people, walking their trails, observing their life, I left the jungles somehow a changed person. Never again could I think of such tribes as being primitive. These were a sophisticated people who might not have my needs for a technological existence, but were certainly meeting their needs in a peaceful and ecologically intelligent way while thoroughly enjoying their life on Colombia's frontiers.

And in a day when indigenous people from the United States to the Amazon to the African plains to the Australian outback have been systematically pushed off their traditional homelands and robbed of all they possessed, Bruce Olson has managed to preserve for the Motilone 95% of their tribal land in Colombia—83,000 hectares—making it one of Colombia's largest reservations. They have developed eight tribal centers within this area—about a day's walk apart. There are 17 graduate nurses who staff each center's clinic. Vaccination and preventative medicine programs have almost controlled the TB and measles epidemics—a perennial problem among indigenous peoples who are newly exposed to carriers from the West. Their population— estimated at 45,000 at the turn of the century— hit a nadir of 3,000, but now the tribe is growing again and has 5,000 people in it.

Bruce has also promoted a cooperative whose center is on the banks of the River of Gold. It serves not only the Motilone tribal members who bring their produce down from their mountain valleys, but also their Colombian neighbors who farm nearby. The co-op has five goals: developing tropical agriculture, managing a farm cooperative store, providing medicine for the Motilone clinics, supporting the six bilingual schools established for the Motilone in the area, and providing necessary advocacy with the government to protect their tribal rights.

The farm cooperative has been very successful in allowing 100 Motilone families who are members to interface peacefully with 40 Colombian farm families who have joined their tribal cooperative, creating a bridge between these once-warring factions. It also lets the Motilone be self-governing and have more power in their local business transactions.

The cash crop of the co-op is cacao which grows wild in the area. A few years ago Bruce began some grafting experiments and developed a hybrid which doubled the size of the native bean— as well as the value of their produce— thus providing the tribe with an easy way to come by necessary cash for purchasing any modern products they may want— knives, schoolbooks, outboard motors for their dugout canoes, clothes to wear when visiting civilization, and even those omnipresent transistor radios.

Though Bruce is a traditionalist who would prefer to see the Motilone live isolated in their thatched longhouses, once the chieftains and the tribe decided they wanted to live in cement block houses, he organized and raised money so that hundreds of Motilone, in the most remote areas, hang their hammocks from composition-roofed, screened-in, cement-block houses. He also agrees that hygienically the thatch houses were impossible to keep free of cockroaches and all those little animals the tropics breed so abundantly. The concrete houses also let TB patients and those with contagious diseases be quarantined, helping to prevent the epidemics which tend to rage through these communities every three or four years. But Bruce strongly encourages each community to keep at least one longhouse to use for their community meetings as a way to preserve their tradition among the tribe.

The Motilone have made gigantic strides in the traumatic process of integrating their culture with the technological society that surrounds them. They have become respected, voting citizens of their state (North Santander) and besides having 400 students studying in their bilingual grade schools situated at various locations on Motilone territory. They also have 15 scholarship students who live in nearby cities during the school year attending secondary schools.

Having these students spend their vacations at home catching up on the know-how and skills of the tribe which they miss learning by being outside the tribe so much is a wise decision. The tribe needs lawyers, nurses and doctors to act as buffers against those who covet their land, yet the tribal people would never respect any male member who had not mastered the tribal arts of hunting, fishing and long-distance running or any female member who didn't know how to weave, garden and prepare their traditional foods.

And it was obvious to me, the day we went fishing with the Motilone, that the students were determinedly trying to keep up with their peers. They knew that these competitive, and sophisticated, hunting and fishing skills meant much to the tribe and that no amount of book-learning would gain them the respect of the community if they did not have a modicum of ability in these areas.

Bruce told me he was early on impressed with the general intelligence level of the Motilone people and how easily they learned new skills. All the motors and modern accoutrements they have acquired in the last two decades are now run and maintained by tribal members.

On the trip back downriver and home, I could only agree as I watched the Motilone pilot of our dugout canoe skillfully handle the outboard motor, moving this long, narrow carved-out tree trunk carrying 14 people through white water rapids and over the rocks in the shallow river. He was serene, watchful, smooth in his movements and exact in his judgments. It was easy to extrapolate and see him in the pilot's seat of a jumbo jet, handling that task with equal aplomb.

The Motilone have named Bruce "Yado" which means "Rising Sun" because of the light he has brought to their tribe. He is a strange mixture of a gentle, tender, friendly man with an iron will and a steely solidarity with the Motilone people. Winsome, yet opinionated, he takes a firm and determined stance in the face of all authority once he has made up his mind. Courageous, with the convictions of a crusader sent to do God's will, he is not moderated by the opinions of established institutions. And there are still Protestant missionaries in Colombia who daily pray for his conversion, feeling he has betrayed the faith of his Christian forebears completely because he will neither build a church nor institute what he considers to be Western forms of Christianity.

Yet he has translated the entire New Testament into their language and the tribe considers itself committed to following Christ to the horizon, although by Western standards they might not appear to have any formal expressions of their faith. At present, according to their age-old customs, there are eight celibate young men who avoid certain foods and are being trained as priests for the tribe. But they plan to build no churches and hold no Sunday morning services. Instead they are learning to be ministers of Christ's gospel in compliance with their traditional indigenous faith forms.

One bilingual Motilone said to me, "Why should we sit in a line in a building for one hour each week to worship God, when I worship God daily walking the jungles, singing my song of faith. It is in the jungles that we expect to hear God. The wind of prophecy that rustles through the trees has always given us the answers of life, suffering and death."

There have been people who have accused Bruce of being either a gold prospector, an emerald smuggler or a person with a messianic complex. I suppose it says something about our Western culture that it is hard to believe someone would do what Bruce has done if he wasn't in it for the money or for the glory. However, he has spent 20 years enduring hardships and isolation, and though physically strong, he has gone through bouts of malaria, dysentery and hepatitis and presently has the dreaded Chagas disease which periodically attacks his body, paralyzing and even blinding him for short periods of time. Although he is under the care of some of the world's eminent tropical medicine experts, still Bruce realizes that of necessity his job is going to be taken over by others some day and he is preparing himself and the Motilone for that time.

When I left the Motilone, I was glad that alongside the horror stories heard around the world of how indigenous peoples are being treated by destructive modern civilization, the story of the Motilone appears to be almost a miracle.

There is also inspiration and hope here for any who strive to work for justice. One person can stand up and make a difference. Bruce Olson can be a model for us all as we contemplate American companies around the world excusing their inhuman behavior in order to satisfy their own greed for other people's property. I can no longer pass a Texaco gas station without wondering how the faceless decision to firebomb the Motilone was justified by some now-forgotten, official in the company.

Our country was founded on the principle that everyone has the intrinsic right to life, liberty and the pursuit of happiness. Yet it is always a mystery to me how so often we have instead pragmatically adopted the imperialistic and despotic practices of George III. Whenever we have power— technological skill or modern weapons— we justify making economic serfs or slaves of the voiceless, little people of the earth— taking away their life and liberty and precluding their ability to pursue happiness.

If God's law really is operative so that you reap what you sow, then it is no wonder Americans are reaping such problems with their oil industry, their inflation and their unemployment! How can we expect otherwise when we have closed our eyes to such immoral behavior by our American business executives around the world? We even excuse such behavior calling it development of the Third World.

The Motilone and their life-style have convinced me that if we are to remain true to our American heritage, and to our Christian ideals, we must begin holding public companies accountable for their malicious lack of ethical standards and seeing that our politicians are not bought by the big moneyed interests so that they implement policies around the world disregarding the human rights of *all* people to life, liberty and the pursuit of happiness. I am thankful for people like Bruce Olson who have obeyed the call of God to go to the far reaches of our planet and be Christians in deed as well as in the word they preach.

Chapter _____ 8

A Rio *Favela* Parish

I woke up and looked at my watch: 5:30 AM. Already the day had begun for many neighbors who seemed intent on letting me enjoy their transistor radios secondhand. The noises and smells of Rocinha— Rio de Janiero's largest *favela* (slum) — begin early. Shortly after the tropical sun starts to paint bright colors into the grey night scene, the crowing roosters, children's cries and neighboring radios pounding out loud, repetitive music begin to compete with one another in the crescendoing din.

Soon the summer heat steams the fetid smell from the omnipresent garbage and open sewers so as the sun rises higher in the sky the stench becomes stronger and ever more offensive. I woke up slowly, trying to mask the happiness inside— knowing I would shortly be leaving, going back to a quiet, sweet-smelling world of running water, electricity, soap and towels— still feeling guilty because I knew that my host and hostess and all the others who lived in this slum had virtually no hope of ever leaving their economic prison.

In all my travels, I had never spent the night in a more noxious place. Yet I had asked to stay the night here because I knew that only then could I empathize even slightly with the thousands who are condemned here for life.

Years before I had decided that Rio de Janeiro was the world's most beautiful city. There long, lazy beaches curve beneath swaying palm trees and a backdrop of craggy mountains covered with tropical vegetation. Magnificent rocks from the same chain as the famous Sugarloaf Mountain add a sense of power to the scene. I'm not the only one who has reached this conclusion, for all this breathtaking beauty makes Rio a jet set mecca.

Of course I had also always known that Rio is a lot more than a playground for the world's elite. Between the gorgeous beaches and the mountains at their back, there lies a narrow strip of land where six million people are crammed and stacked and jumbled in what is considered the world's noisiest city.

Since there simply is not enough land to house all these people, fully a third of Rio's inhabitants— some two million people— live in the *favelas*. These shantytowns tend to be perched on the hills ringing the city. The terrain there is too steep to accommodate regular housing, so squatters with no place to lay their head find what slopes are available for first putting up a crude, homemade tent of cardboard, tin or sacking. Soon this is reinforced with scrap lumber and scavenged building material until there is a whole community of crude shacks which cling together helter-skelter, trying to keep from clattering down the mountainside onto the luxurious modern high-rise apartments and palatial estate homes below. When the winter rains come, invariably hundreds of people throughout Rio find their shacks washed down the hillside. Usually there are fatalities among the young, the weak and the infirm, but there is little leisure for mourning in such communities, and soon these become mere numbers added to the story of the erosion of Rio's mountains.

Life in the favelas is so precarious it is easy to develop a live-laugh-and-be-merry-for-tomorrow-you-may-die attitude. It is the people of the *favelas* who create those fabulously colorful, bespangled costumes and organize the samba schools which make Rio's annual Carnival event a major tourist attraction. Each year some of the world's most privileged come to play with some of the world's most underprivileged.

But most of the time those who live in the *favelas* are forgotten. The opulent homes of Rio's rich, literally within a stone's throw of this slum area, are staffed by maids and gardeners from the *favelas*. In fact most of the workers and service industry employees in Rio live in the *favelas*, and in many ways these people form the economic backbone of the city. Yet officially the *favela* dwellers do not exist for eleven months out of the year.

There are no city services offered them— thus rubble and dusty garbage fill their streets— a sad euphemism for the dirt tracks that run past their hovels. A few shacks in the *favelas* have pirated electricity which is sold them through an intermediary, which means they have to pay more for it than those who live in the official city. Since this electricity is never installed properly, it normally produces about half-strength current. Virtually no one in the *favelas* has running water in their homes. Children and young girls and mothers constantly carry water in every conceivable bottle and pail up the hill from some public spigot at the base of these hills. So in reality the *favelas* cost the city very little for upkeep, yet the workers who live here keep the city going.

I will always remember the first day I walked the beach at Copacabana. I had been in Brazil for seven years but the press of raising ten children plus my other mission duties had never provided me the opportunity of seeing this fabled city. And it does indeed have a sparkle and personality that makes it seem as though people you pass on the streets are on the verge of dancing or singing or playing. Maybe this holiday spirit is generated by the city's many beaches which seem just around every corner. It is hard to take business too seriously when virtually every window looks out on the sparkly ocean. And there is always someone walking past those office buildings in swim attire, carrying an umbrella and a beach bag. Even though you might not be on vacation, since taking advantage of the beaches seems to be a way of life here, it somehow gives you the feeling that soon you *will* be on vacation.

Having come to Rio from the landlocked interior, I immediately caught the fever. It took me only minutes to decide to join the beach throng and I soon was strolling in the warm breezes of the famed Copacabana beach. Suddenly I glanced toward the long row of modern first-class hotels and beautifully accoutered high-rise apartments which line the entire length of the beach— and there between two of these towering buildings I caught a glimpse of the mountain behind, which was virtually covered with ramshackle hovels made of anything that could be stuck together to keep the elements at bay.

This juxtaposition has always seemed to me a poignant statement of conditions in Brazil—where the poor and the servants grovel and cling to a precarious existence in plain view of the wealthy who maintain their opulent life-style because the labor laws do not require them to pay even a living wage to those who work for them. Sad to say, the missionary community becomes party to this system.

When I first went to Brazil I think I was too young to stand up to the old hands, but I never felt quite comfortable with the rationalization that we couldn't pay the people who worked for us more than the going rate because it would ruin the local economy. Seeing the disparity between our own standard of living--which was certainly meager—and the standard our employees could afford on the salary we paid them, it struck me as un-Christian. Such a local economy *needed* to be ruined. But when I campaigned for a change I was told not to rock the boat with radical ideas.

The older I got, the more convinced I was that if we are to live in community with our fellow Christians, then it becomes important that we are not co-opted by an unjust system. Missionaries would tell me that Jesus never tried to change the economic system—he was only interested in changing hearts. But I soon decided they were engaging in sophistry and what I call a selective and sinful reading of the Gospels. Christ put an incredible amount of energy into meeting the physical needs of the people around him—he fed the multitudes, healed the sick, set up the Good Samaritan over against the church leaders as the model we should follow, and told us that giving a drink to the thirsty and feeding the hungry in Christ's name is better than sounding pious or even preaching in Christ's name.

In fact, Christ was very explicit in answering the ones being judged who ask, "Lord, when did we see you hungry or thirsty, a stranger or naked, sick or in prison, and did not come to your help?"

Christ's answer condemns us all: "I tell you solemnly, insofar as you neglected to do this to one of the least of these, you neglected to do it to me." What is worse for us is to learn that those guilty of this crime "will go away to eternal punishment" (Mt 25:44-46). Strong words. It used to worry me to see how much the missionary community was willing to risk eternal damnation—neglecting the hungry, the naked, the sick and the imprisoned who surrounded them on every hand. And how little effort they expended in even reaching out to the impoverished segments of society!

Every year or so I try to return to Brazil to see my family and also to handle publishing business, because during my last half-dozen years in Brazil I began a small publishing house which is still flourishing and needs periodic attention. On a recent trip to Brazil, through these publishing contacts, I met Cristiano Camerman, a Jesuit priest from Belgium who had lived and worked in Rocinha, one of Rio's famous slums, for over seven years. I was intrigued by his willingness to live in a slum and began plying him with questions about his work. Finally, since I knew *favelas* are difficult to visit without some entree, I asked Cristiano if he could possibly arrange this for me. He agreed and even thought that an elderly couple in his parish would be willing to put me up for the night since I wanted to get a full dose of *favela* living.

So it was arranged: I was to be in Rio for a day the following week and would meet Cristiano at the end of his workday in downtown Rio and then follow him through his evening rounds. This would give me intimate contact (at times I was to find it almost too intimate!) with his parishioners—the shantytown dwellers of Rocinha.

The *favela* of Rocinha has about 100,000 people in its jammed-together shacks, perilously situated over a mile-long tunnel which gives access from the rest of the city to one of Rio's famous beaches. Since Rocinha cannot afford to support a parish priest, every day Cristiano joins the streams of workers who come down out of their squatters' shacks perched on every slope of the hills surrounding Rio—overseen by the magnificently tall statue of Christ blessing the city below with outstretched arms from his perch atop Rio's famous Corcovado Mountain.

Cristiano is a trained professor of economics, so he makes his living working for the Brazilian Council of Bishops doing sociological studies at the behest of various bishops. The church leaders in Brazil have found what is true in many other countries of the Third World: by falsifying social statistics, governments attempt to cover up worsening economic and social conditions of the growing impoverished classes. The authorities don't want such adverse publicity to add to the disquiet of the people—as though you need statistics to make you feel better about not being able to find a job. In any case, more and more church leaders around the world are conducting their own sociological studies, hiring academics like Cristiano, to provide statistical evidence which they use as they try to lobby governments into providing justice for their disenfranchised parishioners.

Many of the people in the *favelas* of Brazil's cities have been pushed off lands that have traditionally belonged to them. Through one ploy or another—high taxes, agricultural loans which a bad crop makes it impossibile to repay, or outright land grabbing-- millions of Brazil's peasant farmers have lost their land to foreclosure. Since this land tends to fall into the hands of large conglomerate agribusinesses who concentrate on mechanized farming, these peasant farmers have nowhere to go. Then with no land they not only lose their means of livelihood, but they have no social security, no access to health care and no educational advantages. The only thing they know how to do is subsistence farming, but since that means they don't contribute meaningfully to the world market economy or to the gross national product, the government sees them as expendable.

These are the people who are Cristiano's parishioners. Everyone I talked to in this throbbing community had come to Rocinha from some farming community in the interior. Some had been there for over 20 years. It is quite a parish for Cristiano and his co-worker, Paulo Schweitzer, another self-supporting Jesuit from Belgium. There are 250 children in catechism classes and two masses on Sunday with 1,200 people attending these services. Besides these traditional parish functions, Cristiano and Paulo are involved in myriad programs, which means that virtually every night of the week they are at some community-connected function.

Visiting Rocinha I found fascinating. After rendezvousing in downtown Rio, Cristiano and I had joined the rest of the 6 o'clock commuters on the crowded buses for a 20-minute bus ride home. It was a hot and muggy summer afternoon, and the breeze coming in through the open windows of the speeding bus brought a little relief. My camera was firmly tucked away. Cristiano had made a point of stressing that I should do as little as possible to look like a tourist—that would only invite hostility from the *favela* dwellers who naturally resent being the objects of idle curiosity. It is bad enough to suffer without providing amusement for wealthy tourists who have no idea what it is like to live without hope.

From the bus stop at the end of the tunnel, Cristiano and I climbed part way up the hill to the Community Center the parish has acquired—a rented storefront with apartment above. Cristiano's first meeting of the evening was to take place here.

As a building it wasn't much. Basically grubby, its water-spotted walls bespoke a roof with major leaks. A Ping-Pong table in the corner stood alongside a foot-shuttle sewing machine used by the women in the community for their sewing class. We sat on home-made benches around a table of rough boards atop some sawhorses under a 100-watt bulb which gave off a feeble light because of the secondhand electricity. The heat made me bring out my trusty Chinese fan.

Outside on the narrow street (one of the few in the area where cars could pass), the noise was an incredible cacophony of racing, mufflerless cars and motorcycles. In a ditch in front of the center was a gutted VW bug setting on rusty, wheel-less axles. Leaning against one fender was a tire—someone had thought better of it and left it to rot alongside the rest of its corpse. A young boy went by pushing a homemade wheelbarrow with the squeakiest wheels I'd ever heard. Slowly it squealed all the way down the street to the water spigot. There was a surcease of the grating noise while its containers were loaded up, but soon it started again as the barrow came slowly screeching back up the hill.

None of the nine young men who met here at 7 PM seemed to mind the noise pollution. They were discussing the progress of the program they led. Twice weekly they were gathering boys aged ten to twelve off the street to teach them handcrafts that would give them income from legitimate source—as well as develop a feeling of community amongst them. The leaders, most of whom have had experience in street gangs, know that developing positive peer pressure is a powerful tool to help keep these youngsters from turning to crime and becoming marginalized from society.

While the boys' club planning session was going on, I was taken in tow by Zenith who was going to be my hostess and had come to meet me. As part of the steering committee of the Community Center, Zenith was proud of what they themselves had been able to accomplish and wanted to show me around. The apartment upstairs had been converted into a child care center. Started by women of the community, it allows working mothers in the community to leave their children in responsible surroundings.

Altogether there are about 500 people whose lives are touched by some type of Community Center activity each week. Long ago the people realized that no one in the government cared about Rocinha. So if anyone was to solve their problems they would have to organize themselves and cause it to happen. Cristiano thus spends a lot of his time as a catalyst, helping the people of Rocinha discuss their situation and decide what they need to do about find-ing solutions.

When the planning session ended, Zenith and I followed Cristiano down the most filthy street I'd ever seen to a whitewashed church which stands in stark contrast to much of the dilapidation around it. Last year the people of the community rebuilt the chapel. Its spotless walls and Spanish-tiled floor are a public statement about what the church means to Rocinha.

The Sanitation Committee of 20 people gathered at eight for their weekly meeting to discuss the progress of the sewage issue. It isn't hard to agree with their consensus that water and waste are the two most pressing problems of the *favela*. Although they still did not quite believe it, the committee had managed to spur the government into starting a solid waste processing plant in their slum. Construction had already begun on a site at the base of Rocinha's hill. The timeliness of the election year coming up and the politicians' growing awareness of the tremendous clout wielded by these voting slum dwellers were obviously the main stimuli, in their opinion.

What ensued was an informed dialogue among these committee members, who with little formal education seemed quite savvy about what they had been able to accomplish and how they needed to keep the government locked into producing this definitive action for their *favela*.

The discussion turned to four women who had come to the meeting with a special petition. Their homes had slid down the mountainside in torrential rains the month before. Government representatives, out to inspect the damage the following day, had publicly promised these homeless families that within a week they would begin to build them adequate, permanent shelters. A month had gone by and nothing had happened.

Someone suggested getting mass media coverage to pressure the government to act. A debate ensued regarding how much TV coverage in the past had actually benefited anyone in a concrete way. Cristiano's comment was insightful: "If the government cannot solve the problem of these four families, it is clear to me that they must be either grossly incompetent or uninterested."

Until then Cristiano's calm demeanor had made him appear mild-mannered and easygoing to me. This vehement statement showed that he carries a lot of buried anger about the treatment of his parishioners. Later in discussing this he related how incredulous his parents were when they visited him from Belgium. According to their European viewpoint they simply could not comprehend why the government had allowed this sewage problem to persist in the middle of a sophisticated city for over two decades.

To me the committee members were most cordial and seemed eager to share their concerns and views, making me feel welcome in their midst. They appreciated my interest in their plight, and each one wanted to tell me their own personal story—how they had experienced one reversal or another that had finally landed them in this slum. The night was still steamy hot, so someone slipped out to buy cold pop. Soon there was almost a party savor to the gathering. I was struck by the fact that though these people might have few of the comforts of Western civilization, they had caught the Rio spirit and were wringing as much enjoyment out of life as their circumstances possibly allowed.

Zenith had also come to the Sanitation Committee meeting and displayed a certain proprietorship about my personhood. I was her guest and she was showing me off. She and her husband, Nestor Viana, were considered pillars of the parish who had lived in Rocinha for 24 years. Her attitude helped the others be as gracious as they were, for Zenith's acceptance of me meant that I was part of their community—no questions asked.

After the meeting Cristiano walked Zenith and me up the hill. We climbed steep, uneven steps, ducking under archways and around hovel after hovel through a labyrinth of alleyways to get to the Viano home. Many people were lounging along our pathway— outside their own doorways for the most part—trying to get a breath of fresh air out of the still, hot night. There is little in the *favela* to entertain the populace. No wonder the Community Center was such a hit.

Huffing and puffing from the steep climb, we arrived at Zenith and Nestor's house—a narrow space between two neighbors. A very small dining room/living room combination contained a sofa, a chair and a small table with four chairs. There was a kitchen at the rear of this central living space, and just beyond a plastic curtain door cordoned off the only bedroom. Zenith and Nestor had never had children, but they doted on Cristiano as if he were their son, and praised all he had been able to accomplish for the parish in the seven years he had been there.

We sat around the small, crude table covered by a brightly printed oilcloth with a vase of plastic flowers—adding color and a feeling that my hosts wanted to brighten up their surroundings. Over glasses of lukewarm tea, we discussed the theme that increasingly fascinated me: how one person's effort can make a big difference for a community like Rocinha. Cristiano's role as catalyst was greatly appreciated. He not only had helped the *favela* dwellers articulate their needs and their problems, but also had given them hope that through community effort they could resolve these. The boys' clubs helped with the delinquency problems, the girls' sewing class gave them opportunities to better their situations, the child care center provided help for working mothers, and now the sewage plant offered a relief from the noxious living conditions.

Zenith and Nestor were a great couple—wise with having to cope, happily adjusted to this life with no amenities, few comforts, little privacy. After Cristiano went down the hill to his own digs, we stayed talking late that night and they, too, told me their history and how they'd come to Rocinha. For over 20 years they had lived in this bathroomless shanty simply because they could never afford anything else. Zenith had worked 17 years for a wealthy German family as a maid—almost like one of the family, she explained. Nestor had been an embassy chauffeur when Rio was still Brazil's capital. Now they were both retired, but Zenith dedicated her time and energy at the child care center doing an excellent job as one of the chief administrators there.

Their only source of water stood in the corner of the kitchen—a 50-gallon drum they filled from a nearby stream. I slept on the sofa. Since privacy is a rare commodity in the *favela* no one thought it strange that I should have none. Besides, it made me feel like a member of the family. Shortly after I woke up the next morning a neighbor came by, excited because the spring was uncommonly clean. Nestor hurried out with pails to get in on the bonanza of clean water. Usually the water is grey and murky with pollution from higher up the hill.

Never did I figure out what served them as a toilet. Instinctively I felt it would be an invasion of their privacy to ask. I have wondered if they didn't offer to show it to me from the same reticence, or because they were embarrassed that they did not have any modern facilities. In any case the combination of the tropical heat plus the ability I had learned in the jungle of coping, made it possible for me to wait and use the toilet in the parish house the next morning where I was expected for breakfast. So what with hygienic necessities combined with so much happening around me, there was no thought about sleeping in the next morning. Shortly before six I found myself dressed and ready for the day. I wondered whether anyone would be up at the rectory when I got there.

There was no need to worry. As soon as Father Cristiano opens the front door of the narrow, small quarters which serve as the parish house in Rocinho to let in the morning sun, the parishioners start pouring in. Jorginho, 9, and Luciano, 7, two of the ten children who live next door, tend to be the first—and they had been there over an hour by the time I showed up. These boys have staked out certain claims on Cristiano: Luciano gets to collect (and sell) the old newspapers and magazines from the house, Jorginho runs errands and buys incidental groceries—a liter of milk, a half-dozen eggs. In return Luciano and Jorginho get to do a lot of snacking at the parish house.

Throughout the day, others come to ask favors or advice or just to share the news of the community. Long ago Cristiano decided it was useless to try to keep office hours in this parish—no one would understand a regimented life or closed doors. When he is in Rocinha, he is available.

To live in Rocinha is to become insensitive to noise and stink and too many people crowded too closely together, with little assurance that the future won't be clouded by a tropical rain washing your shack down the mountainside or a government decree ordering your home bulldozed so that you become a victim swept aside into a statistical report. Both privacy and security are unobtainable luxuries. But Cristiano admits the hardest adjustment for him when he first moved to the *favela* was learning to live with the smell. The lack of privacy and the noise level he could cope with. It took a long time to learn to put up with the stench.

It's a good thing he finally did, however, because Cristiano and Paulo live on a narrow street at the base of Rocinha which is literally paved with garbage. An open sewer runs down the middle of the street. Every four years or so (just before elections), the city sends in a crew of garbage collectors to try to convince the people they are cared for. But they all know it is a momentary fling.

Unfortunately these are the little people, the expendable ones, who have been victimized by a system willing to cast them aside. After breakfast as Cristiano and I traveled back down to the city, we talked about how obvious it is here in Brazil that these hardworking people don't have a better life because they have no power. It's not that they are lazy or unwilling to work or that they want to live on welfare, but rather that the people with the decision-making power know they don't have to offer better wages. There are always millions more people looking for jobs—any jobs, at any wage.

Thus people who run big corporations always prefer high unemployment—it keeps the work force insecure and wage levels low.

Once I asked Dom Helder Camara, the archbishop from northeastern Brazil who has worked so long for the underprivileged in his diocese and has been a Nobel Peace Prize candidate for these efforts, why his parishioners were willing to work for 50-cents a day for large plantation owners. Surely it would be better not to work eleven hours in that grueling tropical sun and earn not enough to buy even the basic beans and rice needed for the family for one day. How could they possibly live on that? Why not better stay home?

Dom Helder's quiet eyes saddened as he answered, "My daughter, when you are starving to death, you don't have the option to stay home and wait for a better offer."

I have been haunted by my short stay in Rocinha and Dom Helder's story. It is much easier when you don't have to look into the eyes of these people and realize they have a dignity given them by God which is being trampled by unjust circumstances. A theologian friend of mine from India was discussing with me recently just what our Christian duty is to the starving of the world. He said that a basic problem, even in his country, is how easy it is to ignore these appalling situations by keeping them out of sight. It is disquieting to have to face the reality of Rocinha, or the northeast of Brazil, or the streets of Calcutta. Much easier to concentrate all my attention on my snug world in suburbia, and worry about getting my children to their soccer practice on time.

But unfortunately because of my travels I know that in reality my high standard of living here in the U.S. is in many ways just as exploitative—making me just as guilty—as that plantation owner in Brazil who pays 50-cents for eleven hours of work in the tropical sun. I can buy bananas cheaply at my supermarket because the banana pickers in Central America are paid inhuman wages. The military dictatorships in their countries forbid any unionization or even agricultural co-ops to be formed so that these pickers have no power to strike or better their lot in life. And sadly our American history shows that we sent the U.S. Marines into Central America to stop the unionization of banana pickers.

My cheap tin cans which allow me to have a convenient life are kept at an inexpensive, competitive market price because the tin miners in Bolivia have no option but to work for less than a dollar a day. They have no unions, medical insurance or health care, so most miners die before they are 40 from lung diseases. Because I have seen their eyes, I find it difficult to appreciate cheap tin cans!

Knowing these things firsthand makes it all the harder for me to hear people tell me they deserve the good life they have because they have worked hard for it. I know the good life I enjoy is based on pure luck of birth: but for the grace of God I would have been born into a peasant family in the interior of Brazil with no hope for education, no hope for medical attention, and in spite of long hours spent slaving underneath a tropical sun, very little hope of surviving long on this planet.

Never will I forget a luncheon I attended here in Pasadena of mostly retired people. I sat across from a stylish, grey-haired woman who made a pleasant aside to the companion next to her when the invocation was announced. "I really don't like to give thanks for my food. It makes me feel as though I don't deserve it!"

At first I was so amazed I could say nothing. But surely she believed what she said, because it is discomforting to *not* believe that and enjoy the life-style we have. Also if we do have to be thankful for our food and all our many blessings, that means logically we should share from our largesse with those less fortunate. It seemed senseless to launch into a discourse about how our high standard of living in this country is bought at the expense of workers who don't have the power in their parts of the world to earn a decent, living wage. Yet, always a missionary, I felt it was incumbent on me to try to explain a little to her during this luncheon why she should have a heart resplendent with extreme gratitude every waking moment. I doubt she heard me, but I know now what Christ meant when he said he was speaking to those who had "ears to hear".

We might not see the poor of this world in their destitution, but just as Christ condemned the religious leaders of his day for averting their faces when they saw the wounded by the road, so we too are going to be condemned because we keep the destitute out of our line of vision. Making them invisible lets us think we are relieved of the burden of caring for their plight. But we aren't!

I left Rocinha feeling awe for this gentle priest who is willing to live surrounded by squalor and all it brings, in order to reach out and help those people there that need him so. In a world where it seems as though no one with any power cares, Cristiano brings an incarnated hope to this *favela*. Even though the people there might be marginalized from society in many ways, they know that for

Cristiano they are at the center. He really cares to help them improve their lot. And the active participation of the people in solving their own problems gives them a feeling of self-worth because they are being used as instruments of progress for their own community.

Interestingly enough, by the time I was walking towards the bus stop to leave, somehow I already felt differently towards Rocinha. The smells along the street—the open sewer and fetid garbage— were just as nauseous, but somehow a spark of hope was flaming. Just then a bright-eyed, pretty child in a freshly ironed dress, walked by. She obviously had just come from a bath and walked by on her way to school, wafting a sweet smell of violets along her path.

I was thankful for the trips that allowed me to meet people like Cristiano who are willing to work and strive to make hope a constant factor in that child's life. I was also glad I had seen the plight of the people in Rocinha. I knew I could never stop reaching out to the hungry, the sick, the naked around me, for until justice reigns on this earth all who would follow Christ have a commission to feed, clothe and minister to the poor.

Chapter _____ 9

Central America and Feudalism Revisited

Flying over Central America on a clear day, you tend to be overwhelmed by the majestic beauty of that part of the world where smoking volcanoes surround you on every hand. The plane skirts around one after another of the plumes that waft heavenward signaling a molten mountain beneath. On the slopes of the more dormant volcanoes you can see small farms which march up their sides—volcanic ash reputedly makes very fertile soil—and you find yourself trying to imagine what it must be like to live in the shadow of such ominous power, as well as with the insecurity of being that close to imminent destruction like that which struck 23,000 people in Amero when Nevado del Ruiz errupted recently in Colombia.

But it doesn't take long in Central America to discover that in much of that area, no matter how far you are from the closest volcano, most everyone is equidistant from imminent destruction. Everyone is living on the brink—not necessarily of a volcano—but no one knows when and where death will strike next. Unfortunately most danger doesn't come from natural disasters, but rather from the armed military forces who claim they are ridding the countryside of rebels or Communist guerrillas.

In the past few years several trips have taken me to El Salvador, Nicaragua, Costa Rica, Honduras and Guatemala, and on each journey I have found myself asking a lot of questions about this troubled land. As I experienced too close at hand the violence and mayhem one prefers to read about calmly in the morning newspaper sipping orange juice, I was overwhelmed by the statistics I kept hearing: 40,000 murdered in Guatemala during the last four years, probably the same amount in El Salvador, atrocities being committed against the indigenous population throughout, memories of the bloodbath under Somoza in Nicaragua.

My internal newspaper kept bannering the headline: *10,000 Assassins at Large!* For if, as authorities estimate, over 100,000 people have been wantonly murdered in Central America during the last decade, then you could probably assume there are at least 10,000 people implicated in these crimes. But how does a society produce so many immoral people?

A few years ago I was in embroiled Guatemala, whose story in many ways is typical of the region. Arriving in Guatemala City I was picked up at the airport by my friend Eliana who has worked several years with the aid agency for which I had come to consult. As Eliana deftly maneuvered her way through the heavy city traffic, an army jeep swerved in front of us. Four very young teenagers were seated in the back, carrying semiautomatic rifles pointed out the open tailgate. One youngster, with a mocking smile on his face, carefully swung the barrel of his gun so it was pointed straight at my eyes—five yards away.

I wanted to scold this smart-aleck kid because I knew he was trying to intimidate me. Instead, I turned my head slowly and tried to concentrate on what Eliana was saying. It was apparent to me that I probably had looked into the eyes of one of those 10,000 assassins I was pondering! But it also was clear to me that this was no game and I, too, had been cowed into submission.

Eliana obviously was no stranger to such overt acts of harassment and threatened violence, but she told me that after awhile you must simply learn to ignore the bullies if you are to survive within range of that human volcano! Having observed what Pol Pot's young killers were able to wreak in Cambodia/Kampuchea, and basically convinced of the original sin to be found in all humanity, I wasn't all that surprised to be accosted in this emotional way by the young thug, but I couldn't understand the system which not only harbored him but provided him license.

Later as we drove down a country road to visit some of the aid agency's projects, two armored tanks rumbled past us. I asked Eliana why the semblance of war? She said that the situation was really improved. The year before, those tanks would stop cars at random and for no apparent reason commandeer the vehicle, leaving the passengers to go afoot, or else if they were unlucky, one of the soldiers would simply unconscionably kill them, leaving no witnesses to their robbing the car.

After the coup in Guatemala which placed a touted born-again general, Rios Montt, in the presidency, hopes had been kindled that his laudable aphorisms would trickle down and stop the senseless carnage throughout the land. He was still in power during my stay in Guatemala, and I was repeatedly amazed to hear radio programs interrupted by one-minute spot commercials of Rios Montt urging me to be "obedient to parents, teachers, police and those in authority"! After my scary experience coming in from the airport, this left me more than a little worried. Why were Guatemalans told by their president not to question authority in a land where young hoodlums in uniform could intimidate anyone they felt looked weak?

In some respects Guatemala is a unique Central American country since the majority is not Spanish-descended— of its seven million people over four million are Mayan indigenous, speaking myriad dialects, fiercely clinging to their traditional life-style. The women wear beautiful, brightly colored hand-woven skirts with elaborately embroidered bodices. For centuries these tribal people have lived in isolated mountain valleys—where virtually each valley has spawned its own language and distinctive costume.

But this very uniqueness has allowed even more oppression, for since they have never been unified, the indigenous people have easily fallen under the control of the powerful Ladino (Spanish-speaking) families who run the country as a veritable fiefdom. For the past four centuries the Spaniards have dominated the land with a feudal system which has left the indigenous peoples in what a World Bank report calls "a condition of life so limited by malnutrition, disease, illiteracy, low life expectancy, and high infant mortality as to be beneath any rational definition of human decency".

Until their remote land was considered valuable because of newly-discovered mineral deposits under it and the export cash crops that could be grown on it, the Mayan population and their homeland were ignored. The situation, unfortunately, has changed and the powerful feudal forces are now coveting the Mayans' traditional land which now has commercial value.

Calling any Mayans who want title to their own land Communists, one oppressive military government after another has been killing those indigenes who happen to get in the way of their designs—especially concentrating on tribal members who seem to have leadership and organizational skills. The last thing the Guatemalan oligarchy wants is a concerted front on the part of the Mayan people.

Many of the development agencies which work among the Mayans in the hinterlands of Guatemala first came to the country after the devastating 1976 earthquake which killed 40,000 people—mostly peasant farmers and tribal people from the highlands. This disaster was an incredible learning experience for the Mayans because they were forced into working together to rebuild a life out of the ruins in which they found themselves. And these aid agencies helped them bridge the gaps of language and culture that had divided one valley from the next for generations. The rubble thus spawned cooperation and also began to give to these indigenous peoples a feeling of self-worth.

After this disaster the aid agencies stayed on to facilitate development programs which allowed Guatemalans to help each other. Lately, however, these agencies have been pulling out, one by one, because it is ever more dangerous to help the indigenous peoples. In fact, anyone helping the Mayans achieve a status of dignity is seen as an enemy by the Guatemalan hierarchy. One American Catholic missionary, Stanley Rother, from Okarchi, Oklahoma, killed in front of his parish house by Guatemalan government agents, said before his death, "To shake the hand of an Indian is a political act."

Recently a Guatemalan doctor, Juan Jose Hurtado, who in 1976 had spontaneously set up a free clinic to help the indigenous neighbors of his summer home injured in the earthquake, fled the country after having been jailed as a Communist sympathizer. His friends and neighbors acknowledge that Dr. Hurtado had never involved himself in politics. But after that first earthquake crisis Hurtado continued to keep the clinic open—spending weekends meeting the medical needs of his Mayan neighbors. In the process his humanitarian work received international recognition—which finally saved him—because when he disappeared, pressure from international groups such as Amnesty International managed to free him. Without this outside help he probably would have gone the way of many other small people who try to help the Mayans: disappearing without a trace into the murky abyss of the Guatemalan death squads.

I went with Eliana to visit one of the few remaining development projects in the country. We twisted our way up the scenic side of Agua Volcano (Water Volcano) which has kept its name even though 200 years ago an earthquake split the volcano sending the contents of its famed crater lake crashing down on thousands of people living in the pleasant valley at its feet. There is no more lake, the volcano is quiet, the towns are all rebuilt, and the farms are back on the slope of the mountain.

In the hamlet of Santa Clara Corquin I met Juana Menchu, an indigenous woman in her colorful, handwoven skirt. She stood outside her home—a thatched-roof hut on the rural slope—and pointed out the two orphans, aged six and eight, added to her family two months earlier. Their parents, distant relatives, had been massacred before the children's eyes along with 200 other villagers—women, men, the aged and the infants—in the neighboring district of Chimaltenango, supposedly for the crime of selling their corn to guerrillas.

Many feel this is just an excuse, however, since the army is enflamed by the belief that a live peasant is a potential landowner or a potential leftist guerrilla and is attempting militarily to clear a battle zone of all inhabitants—either by forcibly relocating those they consider intransigent to refugee camps in safe zones or by killing them. Both solutions are cruel and unnecessary.

The army also then implements a scorched earth policy—burning crops and buildings, making it difficult for other Mayans to settle on their traditional land, but leaving it nicely cleared for the large landowners who have their eyes on moving in with their mechanized farming methods when the area is cleared of guerrillas. Thus those with power who are greedy for more property are using creative means to push these virtual serfs off their land.

This is true throughout the region. The undeclared war in El Salvador heated up when in order to qualify for U.S. aid the government instituted land reform and promised the peasants their own farm plots from immense haciendas.

Dona Juana has never been to school and can't read, but she has a sophisticated understanding of her community's situation. I asked her what she considered to be her greatest need.

Without hesitating a moment she responded, "Land! There's plenty of land here, we just can't cultivate it."

Juana and her husband earn $1.50 or $2.00 a day as day laborers for a neighboring Ladino farmer, even though the legal minimum is $3.70. In spite of her illiteracy and being what many would call a simple, indigenous peasant women because she has no *formal* education and no economic power, Juana impressed me with her poise and inward dignity.

I queried her further about the land she was convinced would solve her community's problem: She knew precisely how much corn they could cultivate per year and mustered her arguments to prove to me that if the people of her village could only have access to small acreages of tillable land they could support themselves.

But the story is the same here as in Brazil: since subsistence farming does not add to the export market or to the GNP of the country, these people are seen as expendable by those in power— whose goals are to become potent operators on the world market. And their problems do not interest those who govern. Yet in one aspect these people in Santa Clara are lucky— if they *had* land they would sooner become targets of the death squads or the power plays by some strong-arm coveting their property.

For 400 years Juana's ancestors have struggled to preserve remnants of their Mayan heritage and also establish a life-style with a modicum of dignity; yet she and her community continue to live under a feudal system which gives them no chance to land ownership. Her village is obviously impoverished. Everyone in it lives in a thatched hut, as does Juana's family, and they all work as day laborers for neighboring landholders.

The hamlet is more fortunate than many for they have a school— built by a group from a church in Canada who came one summer to construct this gathering place for the community. The children weren't in school the day I visited because the state-supported teacher had shown up drunk again that morning and the mothers had sent him packing. Some of the children were helping their mothers husk corn and prepare it for making the local variety of tortillas. Others were tending the younger toddlers.

There is no running water in the village, so the children tend to be grubby from playing in the dirt made dusty by the fine, greyish volcanic ash which falls practically daily, spewed from the smoldering crater above. This ash is apparently very unhealthy to breathe constantly, but since it is like a fertilizer from heaven and since these indigenous people are needed to work on the hilly farms, no one tries to warn them of the dangers inherent in the land.

But, sadly this volcanic ash presents a minimal danger when compared to other poisons loosed on the countryside by agribusiness in Guatemala. Noam Chomsky and Edward Herman in their book *The Political Economy of Human Rights* state that the high cotton yields in Guatemala are due to the dangerous level of insecticide spraying that is practiced—the highest in the world—by corporations with virtually no concern for the million Guatemalans who either work the fields or live nearby.

Their book also reports studies showing the unsafe level of DDT in mothers' milk in Guatemala—up to 185 times higher than the safe limit—and explains how meat which is rejected for shipment to the U.S. because of its high DDT content is sold locally or in the Caribbean. Again, the victims of these policies have virtually no political voice, so these issues are not even raised in the local journals. It is no wonder that the age expectancy for those living on the slopes of the volcanos is about 35 years.

Leaving Santa Clara and Agua Volcano, I thought of the blood that was shed 500 years ago by our own ancestors in their attempts to throw off feudalism. The peasants then, with not enough food, no land, forced conscription, no education and no hope of ever changing their status, decided that fighting to the death was preferable to slow starvation from slaving under feudal lords with no access to education or health care.

No wonder the peasants today in much of Central America who face the same conditions see guerrilla rebellion as the only recourse in their oppressed condition. I am always amazed at how North Americans, whose ancestors fought against the same kind of cruel overlords and died to give us the freedoms we now possess, can provide military assistance to help the modern feudal lords acquire sophisticated firepower and means of extortion which make the battle hopelessly one-sided.

While I was in Guatemala, 18 Mayans seized the Brazilian consulate to protest the cruel treatment of the indigenous peoples in their country. It amazed me to find out later, not through the world media which apparently thought this unnewsworthy information, that these "Communist guerrillas" were all women and were armed only with Molotov cocktails and one 22-caliber pistol. But they were desperate to communicate to the world the plight of their people.

Humanitarian agencies have had little success in Guatemala and El Salvador—countries of seven and five million people respectively—in stopping the carnage of the last few years. Everyone I met on the trip had someone in their immediate family who had disappeared or had been tortured, raped or murdered in this burgeoning terror—Eliana's uncle and two cousins; Juana's distant relatives whose children she has befriended plus three cousins tortured and killed. The stories were hard to listen to—so many tears, so much heartache. Yet bearing one another's burdens meant trying to communicate to them that I cared.

And this feudal system which has existed in Central America for the past four centuries is being defended by the military oligarchy with the help of U.S. military advisers and U.S. tax dollars. One Guatemalan president was quoted as saying he is willing to suppress what he terms a peasant revolt even "if it takes 100,000 lives". The American government, with a declared motivation of creating stability in the area, promised military aid to this crazed leader.

So what does the church say in such a situation? Unfortunately saying anything is dangerous. Many of the religious community are paying a high price to heed Christ's call to feed, clothe and visit "the least of these" in Central America. Clergy and missionaries throughout the area either have fled for their lives or have been victims of the senseless killing. Their crime has been to speak against the injustices of the system.

One case in point is the 1978 Panzos Massacre in Guatemala. For years the indigenous tribe living there had been in extreme isolation, with an occasional outsider penetrating the area—an itinerant Catholic priest who came quarterly to baptize children and bless marriages, or at rare intervals the recruits from the not-too-distant small army post at the end of a dusty dirt road.

In due course Panzos became the target of development. Mineral surveys conducted from the air indicated valuable deposits of oil, besides rare titanium, nickel and uranium to be found here. U.S. AID tax money was invested to build roads that finally made Panzos accessible to civilization. At this, wealthy and powerful people came into the area claiming that the land was theirs and that the indigenous people whose families had been living on it for generations were poachers.

The local Catholic priest, knowing that the law guaranteed to the indigenous people their traditional lands, told them that they needed to apply at the land office for lawful title to their territory to secure it against these ruthless land grabbers. But no matter how they tried to get title to their property, these Mayans were given the red-tape runaround.

Unfortunately the priest underestimated the viciousness and power of these wealthy landowners, so he encouraged the indigenous people to go en masse to the local governor to peacefully petition their rightful due. Since they had advised the governor of their intentions, what happened can only be called a setup: Soldiers opened fire on the unarmed tribal people killing 114 in cold blood. It became gruesomely clear that the land robbers had the army on their side and were planning to rid the area, using any pretext or power play, of any indigenous people who might have rightful claim to this land.

Since the priests of the Catholic church were seen as fomenting rebellion by informing the indigenous peoples of their rights, the Catholic church, too, became a target for the military oligarchy and the ruling families of Guatemala. Small wonder that they chose as president for a time a general converted to a Protestant splinter group. Caesar's old tactic of dividing and conquering still seemed viable, and some observers felt that by dividing the church, those in power hoped to continue their genocide with impunity. However, after Rios Montt publicly demeaned the visiting pope, it was too much even for the generals, so the Catholics are back in office again.

What was fascinating to watch was the linkup between the conservative fundamentalists in the U.S. — who seem to have a basic infatuation with power — and the government of Rios Montt — who catered to the traditionally disenfranchised Protestants in a vastly Catholic society. This resulted in the American president embracing Rios Montt publicly, stating that this murderer has been "given a bum rap" in the American press.

This probably referred to the international observers who were worried when Rios Montt came to power because of his long record of heavy-handed and bloody moves against the indigenous population— he is best known for having directed a massacre in 1973 in San Sirisay, Jutiapa, where more than 100 Mayans were slaughtered. Then in his first six months in office Amnesty International reported that 2,600 people were killed by government forces with no thought to their human rights or a fair trial. Rios Montt claimed that everyone the army killed was a Communist or a Communist sympathizer. To be able to *find* and *kill* that many Communists in a country of only seven million makes his claim unbelievable.

The Central American military's strong stance against critics in the church thus becomes understandable. The church is trying to preach justice and peace to the society and specifically to soldiers involved in these killings. Many believe that Archbishop Romero in El Salvador, who had been a well-known conservative, became vociferously anti-military after several of his priests were murdered. Then it was only two days after going on radio and telling the military to lay down their guns because they were sinning against God by participating in the killing of innocent civilians that he was murdered at the high altar while serving communion. Robert White, ambassador to El Salvador under Carter, has said publicly that he has seen documentation proving that the American-supported right-wing leader, D'Aubuisson, paid a professional assassin to kill the archbishop.

In the face of all this, what is to be done? I left Guatemala on this trip pondering these horrendous problems. I couldn't get that hostile boy in the Jeep playing games with his loaded weapon out of my mind. Why do the oligarchy try to rule by fear— terrorizing any who stand in their way?

I remember meeting Archbishop Romero at the Puebla conference in Mexico in 1979. He knew then he was probably going to be assassinated because he had repeatedly received threats to "shut up or die". Many believe D'Aubuisson is glad it is common knowledge that he ordered the archbishop's death. The lesson is clear: No one is above the melee, nothing is sacrosanct— if you try to limit the oligarchy's power, you will be eliminated.

But how did a society produce all those people willing to kill their neighbors? What social fabric had formed these assassins? Victor Alba, a sociologist from Mexico, claims that 58% of all children in Latin America are born illegitimate— creating a sociological problem with immense ramifications.

Historically the land was invaded by Spanish Conquistadores who came without their wives and treated the local indigenous women as chattel. This pattern has had long-term effects. Few laws today protect the rights of women or children. Most homes have no strong male models in them, so many boys grow up feeling lost and powerless. And as in Kampuchea these youngsters are prime candidates for becoming the agents the military needs to terrorize the countryside. The army issues them guns, gives them a feeling of

importance, and implicates them in dehumanizing crimes—
then as accomplices they are in no position to accuse others of
wrongdoing.

Thus Romero, a respected church leader, was striking a blow at
the basic modus operandi by denouncing these military killings as
sin. He had power over the consciences of the people and had
to be silenced.

Of course the underlying, crucial issue dominating the struggle
is deciding who is going to control the land. It is a feudal struggle
and land is really the crux. In discussing this with Eliana and others
I met in Guatemala, I made the unfortunate comparison to the
equally disturbing moves of the American administration against
the public land in the U.S. The Executive Order selling off over 300
million acres of public property to the private sector during an
economic depression meant that this land was being handed over
to our own wealthy oligarchy.

So land reform in Central America and land reform in North
America began to appear philosophically as two sides of the same
coin. It again comes down to who is able to grab control of the land.
The wealthy few in Central America own the land now and the people
are struggling for access to it, while in North America much of the
public land is in the process of being transferred to the wealthy
few.

Just as I asked, "Why the senseless killings in Central America?"
I also ask, "Why the senseless selling of America's public lands
during a depressed real estate market?" History has taught us that
controlling the land is the first step out of—or into—feudalism.
We should take pause when the governments in Central America
and here in the U.S. are clearly working for the oligarchy with the
aim of putting the control of land into their hands. Democracy
occurs when land ownership is in the hands of a broad base. It is
feudalism to put the major part of property into the hands or
control of a few.

The current land policies of the U.S. administration have been
instituted in the face of a million signatures petitioning against
these objectives. With almost a crazed missionary zeal—irrevocably
transferring as much public land to the private sector as possible—
a neofeudalistic system where the major land holdings fall into the
hands of a few may be visited on our land. Since high interest rates
prevent the middle echelons of American society from borrowing
money to buy houses, let alone wheel and deal in speculative real

estate, it appears that with little hoopla our birthright is being sold out from under us. North and south of the Rio Grande the feudalistic oligarchy, whose wealth is only increased by recessions and high unemployment, continues to acquire control of the land.

These were disturbing reflections which continued during my flight back home. Having more than once felt terrorized by having to pass through armed roadblocks, and knowing the danger of the forays we made into Mayan communities, I was relieved when my plane finally took off from Guatemala City. I was glad that the consulting job was over and that I could go back to my safer spot of the world.

Back home the next morning, as I sipped my orange juice and opened my newspaper, I read that 25 children, 15 women and three men—all Mayan—were found murdered in the mountain hamlet of Saquiya Dos, guilty of collaboration with the guerrillas.

Sadly I shook my head: These are more of those innocent victims of a senseless war that seethes beneath the surface—much like an unpredictable volcano. When will it ever stop?

Where will the next human generated volcano erupt next?

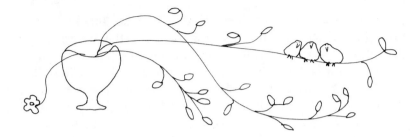

Conclusion

Last week the liturgy in our Sunday service here in Pasadena was based on African religious music. The rector told us that there were twice as many members of the world's 60 million communicating Anglicans in Africa as there were in the U.S. It seemed appropriate therefore that we participate in the worldwide communion by sharing in their liturgical forms.

One of the Ghanaian folks songs which was translated and used in the service somehow summarized all the lessons I have learned from my various trips. The title was, "Jesu, Jesu, Fill Us With Your Love," and the words went on to say,

> Show us how to serve
> The neighbors we have from you. . . .
>
> Neighbors are rich and poor,
> Neighbors are black and white,
> Neighbors are nearby and far away.
>
> These are the ones we should serve,
> These are ones we should love.
> All are neighbors to us and you.
>
> Loving puts us on our knees,
> Serving as though we were slaves;
> This is the way we should live.

That African song says it so clearly: If we are filled with Jesus' love, thereby showing to the world around us that we are truly his disciples, then we will care about our neighbors near and far.

That caring spurred the missionary movement, for when Christians began to care that neighbors they had never seen could hear the message of the gospel, pioneers like William Carey ventured to unknown shores. But this caring must also spur us on today in our work for justice—because if our neighbors are starving to death, they will have no energy to hear that good news that Christ has come to earth to bridge the gulf that now exists between God and humankind.

I have very little confidence in political solutions to the problems faced by the world today. Unfortunately I am old enough to have observed that all power strives to be absolute—and when power becomes absolute it is totalitarian—whether it continues to call itself democratic, socialistic or communistic.

But I do believe we must not be lethargic politically. Christ was not a lethargic person. And like him, we must be willing to speak up for justice—to call the authorities Whited Sepulchres when their actions are evil. There is one great difference, however, between Christ and many of those who have wanted to right the evils of the world—he was not personally interested in assuming a position of power.

Even among Christ's own disciples this was the perennial question—who would have the seat of honor, of highest power? Jesus kept trying to explain to them that they could only be great in his kingdom by serving, and the symbol he used was footwashing--considered the task of the lowliest servant.

That is the secret. We must be willing to be lowly tools in this task of setting up the kingdom. Not looking for positions of honor, but merely reaching out to those near and far. If we ask God to show us what to do for our neighbors, it usually doesn't take long before an opportunity comes our way. The important ingredient is developing a willing heart and listening ears.

We are mandated to feed the hungry, clothe the naked, heal the sick and visit the imprisoned—regardless of whether they are willing to listen to our gospel message. To be a Christian means that we must be ready to be considered the least, "serving as though we were slaves."

Yet the temptations we still face today are the same ones Christ overcame in the desert. After fasting for 40 days, the devil said, "You deserve it—turn these stones to bread."

And today the same temptation comes our way. The devil says to us, "You deserve it. Take the goodies that surround you. The good life is your due."

Since not everyone in the world can live as well as we in North America can, the temptation for us is to justify a luxurious life-style by saying we've come by it honestly. Our parents, our American heritage, our own hard work have all combined to give us the bountiful life we deserve— so please don't bother us with uncomfortable facts about the rest of the world's problems.

This isolationist attitude is tantamount to pledging allegiance to the devil, which was Christ's second temptation. "Buy into my system and I'll give you the world," the devil told Christ. And to put ourselves first is still the basic temptation of humankind.

But "Just Believe in Yourself and Watch Out for Number One" is not the message Christ taught his disciples. Christ's answer to the devil in the wilderness is that, "Humans cannot live on bread alone," or to paraphrase it, "The goodies of this life are not where it's at!"

A careful reading of Scripture would show us that prosperity is never a sign of God's approval. In fact Christ bewildered his disciples so much they even wondered aloud who would get into heaven— because he went so far as to say it is easier for a camel to go through the eye of a needle than for a rich person to get into heaven. The natural conclusion from that awesome statement would be that very few Americans will find it easy to get into heaven! So it behooves us to listen to those lonely voices that cry out to the American church to assume a humbler life-style, to participate in the suffering of our deprived neighbors and to care for the many fallen along the wayside.

Christ's third temptation in the wilderness can also be extrapolated to our modern situation. The devil said, "Show the world that God is on your side. Fling yourself down from the parapet of the temple." And the devil even went on to quote the Bible to prove his case: "Scripture says, 'He will give his angels orders to take care of you', and again, 'They will support you in their arms for fear you should strike your foot against a stone'."

And so the temptation today says, "Be reckless, do your own thing, fling yourself wildly through life, and show the world you can snub your nose at the laws of nature that surround you." And bowing to this temptation, we wildly waste our limited energy resources, expecting some future miracle, some angel ordered to care for us, to keep us from crashing in a disaster. We ignore the laws of ecology, destroying the beautiful earth God has given us, selfishly being reckless with all its natural riches, building industries and plants whose waste products are slowly destroying our gorgeous planet.

Worse, we try to protect our own precious property by putting our energies into arsenals that we hope will keep the enemies whom we have fabricated—or antagonized—at bay. Instead of working for a world of justice without war, without fear and without oppression, where all people are honored and valued as children of God, we prefer to trust in the idols we worship which we have fashioned out of steel and uranium and gunpowder.

A kingdom of love demands that we do not put our priorities on materialistic items nor on being Number One. A kingdom of love demands a world view that puts us in the proper perspective vis-a-vis all our neighbors. And this Kingdom of Love "puts us on our knees, serving as though we were slaves; this is the way we should live."

Faith Annette Sand is a cross-cultural consultant and a publisher who lives in Pasadena, CA with her husband, Albert Cohen, a campus minister at Cal. State L.A. She has a B.A. in history from Wheaton College, IL and an M.A. Missiology from Fuller Theological Seminary, Pasadena. Her interest in missions has led to her publishing numerous articles on related subjects and attending international church conferences from Lausanne, Switzerland to Puebla, Mexico. *Travels of Faith* is the first of a trilogy describing her philosophy and spiritual journey.

ORDER FORM

Travels of Faith

Write— or use this page as a handy order form.

Please send me _____ copies of

Travels of Faith

@ $4.95 each plus postage and handling (95¢ for first book,
35¢ for each book thereafter. *CA residents add 6% tax*).

Mail to:
Hope Publishing House
P.O. Box 60008
Pasadena CA 91106

Send books to:

Name _____

Address _____

City, State, Zip _____

I enclose $ _____ with this order.

HOPE/ISBN 0-932727-03-4 $4.95

Postage
Stamp

to: **Hope Publishing House
P.O. Box 60008
Pasadena CA 91106**

TAPE CLOSED

TAPE CLOSED

TAPE CLOSED

CUT

ORDER FORM

Travels of Faith

Write— or use this page as a handy order form.

Please send me _____ copies of

Travels of Faith

@ $4.95 each plus postage and handling (95¢ for first book, 35¢ for each book thereafter. *CA residents add 6% tax*).

Mail to:
Hope Publishing House
P.O. Box 60008
Pasadena CA 91106

Send books to:

Name _____

Address _____

City, State, Zip _____

I enclose $ _____ with this order.

HOPE/ISBN 0-932727-03-4 $4.95

CUT

Postage
Stamp

to: **Hope Publishing House**
      P.O. Box 60008
      Pasadena CA 91106

TAPE CLOSED

TAPE CLOSED

TAPE CLOSED

ORDER FORM

Travels of Faith

Write—or use this page as a handy order form.

Please send me _____ copies of

Travels of Faith

@ $4.95 each plus postage and handling (95¢ for first book,
35¢ for each book thereafter. *CA residents add 6% tax*).

Mail to:
Hope Publishing House
P.O. Box 60008
Pasadena CA 91106

Send books to:

Name _____

Address _____

City, State, Zip _____

I enclose $ _____ with this order.

HOPE/ISBN 0-932727-03-4 $4.95

CUT

Postage
Stamp

to: **Hope Publishing House**
P.O. Box 60008
Pasadena CA 91106